Teaching Information Writing K–8

JoAnn Portalupi
Ralph Fletcher

Stenhouse Publishers
Portland, Maine

Stenhouse Publishers
www.stenhouse.com

Library of Congress Cataloging-in-Publication Data

Portalupi, JoAnn.
    Nonfiction craft lessons : teaching information writing K–8 /
JoAnn Portalupi and Ralph Fletcher.
        p.   cm.
    Includes bibliographical references.
    ISBN 1-57110-329-5 (alk. paper)
    1. English language—Composition and exercises—Study and teaching
(Elementary)   2. English language—Composition and exercises—Study
and teaching (Middle school)   3. Exposition (Rhetoric)—Study and
teaching (Elementary)   4. Exposition (Rhetoric)—Study and teaching
(Middle school)   I. Fletcher, Ralph J.   II. Title.
LB1576.P659 2001
372.62′3044—dc21   2001017018

Interior design by Catherine Hawkes, Cat & Mouse
Typeset by Technologies 'N Typography

Manufactured in the United States of America on acid-free paper
10 09 08 07 06 05   16 15 14 13 12 11 10

to Don Murray,
who continues to inspire us
with his passion for the craft of writing

Contents

Alphabetical List of Nonfiction Craft Lessons

Acknowledgments

*M*ega-thanks to Brenda Power and Philippa Stratton. In lots of ways, large and small, they were crucial to making this book come alive. They were our first audience, and we are indebted to them.

We are honored to include craft lessons from master teachers: Lisa Siemens, Aimee Buckner, Bev Gallagher, Jane Winsor, and JoAnn Wong-Kam. Thanks!

This book was also nourished by ongoing conversations with our colleagues Ann Marie Corgill, Martha Horn, Lynne Herschlein, Marianne Norman, Franki Sibberson, Artie Voigt, and Cyrene Wells.

Our four boys—Taylor, Adam, Robert, and Joseph—continue to teach us a ton about the power and pitfalls of information writing.

On the videotape "The Writing Workshop: A World of Difference" (Calkins and Harwayne 1987), Martha Horn has a writing conference with a little boy who is writing about trains. "This is a teaching book," he explains with all the purpose and seriousness of a *New York Times* reporter. This book has been inspired by that boy and thousands of young nonfiction writers like him. We have worked with these kids all over the country, and seen up close their intense desire to question, research, understand, and explain the world around them. As much as anything else, they have shown us the enduring importance of this genre.

Introduction

A few years ago we were preparing a big workshop on how to teach nonfiction writing. In our workshops we like to feature lots of student writing. But when we started digging for wonderful, quirky, voice-filled examples of content-area writing, we ran into a snag—we couldn't find much. We had stacks of terrific narrative, fiction, and poetry, but very little wonderful nonfiction writing by students. In an effort to stem a mounting sense of panic, we telephoned Don Graves and told him about our dilemma.

"You know what researchers say when something like that happens," Don said with a chuckle. "No data *is* data."

"You mean—"

"I mean you've got to pay attention to the fact that you don't have many nonfiction samples from students," he said. "That's got to tell you something."

He was right. It wasn't due to chance that we had trouble digging up student nonfiction samples. Rather, this lack indicated a larger problem in our writing classrooms.

For almost twenty years we have been advocates of the writing process approach to teaching writing. We believe that this approach has had a dramatic, highly positive effect on thousands of classrooms. But this effect has been largely limited to expressive writing: poetry, memoir, personal

1

narrative. When we visit classrooms we are often impressed by the quality of student writing in these expressive genres. But other types of student writing—reports, persuasive and expository essays—have not seen a similar transformation. Too often we see the same tired encyclopedia-inspired writing that is so hard to read.

That's where we come in. We see this book as filling the need for teachers who are challenged to teach the kind of writing that draws less on students' stories, memories, and histories, and more on the concrete "out there" world. We bring to this book the same mind-set that we brought to the first *Craft Lessons:* the idea that good writing isn't produced by magic, but by learning to arrange particular words in a particular order to create a particular effect. Such writing doesn't have to be drab, dull, or unreadable. A number of tangible subskills are involved. When we teach students these skills we help them to master a kind of writing that will be crucial as they continue to learn about the world around them.

But let's not forget that we are working with children and young adolescents. Lauren Loewy wrote "All abawt thee oyl sPil" (Appendix C) when she was in first grade, and it really sounds like first-grade writing. She lists a few facts, and isn't shy about expressing her outrage. Her writing has voice. Shelley Harwayne argues that teachers should foster more childlike writing in students, the "kind of writing only they can do." We heartily agree. Where did people ever get the idea that when children write reports they should sound like miniature environmental experts who work for the U.S. government? We need to create classrooms where our students can truly be themselves, where they can bring their passion, knowledge, quirky humor, and authentic voice to this kind of writing.

How to Use This Book

Nonfiction writing is a huge world that encompasses all-about books, scientific writing, biography, reports, how-to, expository, and persuasive writing, feature articles, and much more. When we lived in Alabama our first-grade son learned the technology to make terrific PowerPoint presentations about the planets or endangered animals. In other schools older students have mastered the use of HyperStudio to present information in an engaging format. Tom Romano has expanded the frontiers of content-area writing with his ideas on the "multigenre research paper."

Are we sympathetic to such work? You bet. But in this book we have resisted the temptation to rush headlong into the world of creative nonfiction genres. Although a few of these craft lessons address these, most of them stay pretty close to the meat-and-potatoes content-area writing students do with teachers' guidance on a daily basis.

This book is divided into K–2, 3–4, and middle school (grades 5–8) sections. These divisions, however arbitrary, reflect various differences between emerging, competent, and fluent writers. Not only are middle school students older than second graders, but they also are able to read more challenging texts. And they live in a more demanding curricular world where they will be expected to create more sophisticated and complex nonfiction texts.

We begin each section with a brief introduction to those particular students—their characteristics, quirks, strengths, and passions. You'll notice that each section begins with a handful of "exploratory craft lessons." William Zinsser has written that "students need to learn an unpretentious prose about the world around them." We agree. These exploratory craft lessons focus on how students can write, think, and talk their way into a better understanding of their topics.

Each section contains a wide range of craft lessons. But in each section you'll find a critical mass of lessons directed at the genre that seems most appropriate for that particular age. In the K–2 section, for example, a number of craft lessons focus on the all-about or concept book. In the 3–4 section there are a number of craft lessons pertaining to biography. In the 5–8 section you'll find a series of craft lessons that address expository writing.

Every craft lesson in this book follows the same format:

- **Name** of the craft lesson or writing skill.

- **Discussion** of the lesson, telling why we chose it. Here we talk about the specific need the craft lesson is designed to meet.

- **How to Teach It**—Concrete language a teacher might use to bring the craft lesson to students in either a workshop mini-lesson, individual conference, or small-group discussion. Both authors of this book share a strong distaste for "scripted" teaching. At the same time, we recognize that teaching is an isolating profession. It is our experience that teachers hunger for specific ideas and language they can use as a springboard into their own teaching. We expect and encourage you to take the words provided and tailor them until the craft lesson feels like your own.

- **Resource Material** lists the book or text referred to in the craft lesson. Occasionally we suggest additional texts that can be used to teach the lesson. At times we refer to a passage, poem, or piece of student writing that can be found in the Appendixes.

After the original *Craft Lessons: Teaching Writing K–8* was published, we received this letter from a teacher. She wrote in part:

> Your book made me feel as if there was a wonderful teacher down the hall doing exciting things with her students during writing time. Every day I poked my head into her room and watched how she taught. Sometimes I used her ideas, books for modeling, even her words, exactly as she did. Other times the craft lesson she did sparked an idea for a different craft lesson I could do. The important thing was that I wasn't alone. Her door was open, and I knew I could pop in and observe—and borrow her ideas!— whenever I felt like it.

We hope you'll use this new book in the same spirit.

Setting the Table for Nonfiction Craft

When I (JoAnn) was in fifth grade my teacher assigned each of us a state report. I chose Alaska. Perhaps this state captured my imagination because I loved our snowy Vermont winters. Thirty years later only one thing stands out in my memory of that report: the plywood cover I designed using my brother's wood-burning tool. I stood side by side with my dad in his workshop, and he showed me how to hold the tool steady and move it slowly. I made a picture of an igloo beneath the carefully burned letters that spelled Alaska. I'm sure I spent more time working on that cover than I did on researching and writing the report it held.

We believe others share similar experiences. Student attempts at nonfiction often result in superficial handling of the material. Delving into a topic with a researcher's eye takes time. Many children's first attempts at nonfiction writing happen unintentionally. In the writing workshop students are encouraged to write from their own expertise. Cara's mother is a painter, so Cara writes a book about an artist's studio. Gregory works after school training falcons, so it's natural for him to spin out a piece with facts about these fascinating birds. In both cases, these students are writing what they know, and although they have unintentionally entered the arena of nonfiction writing, they may have little desire to venture deeper into the realm of research. It isn't always necessary for children to back up such narratives with further study, but these early forays into the genre offer a natural invitation for us to introduce students to the process of research.

When I was teaching fourth grade I addressed research writing in two ways. On the one hand, I watched for students like those I mentioned above. When students were writing nonfiction, I often spent one-on-one conference time discussing how to extend their knowledge through further research. On the other hand, I looked for occasions when I could lead the entire class in a genre study on nonfiction writing. One year our writing workshop became a research workshop in which all the students researched individual topics centered around life in colonial New Hampshire. Whether conferring with individual writers or leading the class in a genre study, I had particular "lessons" I wanted to teach my students about the research process.

This book focuses on teaching students elements of craft for nonfiction writing. We would be remiss, however, if we moved directly to the product of student research without taking a brief look at the research process that lays the foundation for writing well in their subjects. We believe students need time to research during the school day, in a workshop setting, where teachers can coach them in the process the same way we coach them as they write. Here are eight pointers to get you started. We encourage classroom teachers to incorporate these ideas into their workshops as they guide students into the exciting world of research.

Find the Right Topic

For some students, finding the right topic is easy. When our niece Rebecca was fourteen she decided to change her eating habits and become a vegan. Most of us in the family needed her to teach us what this meant. That wasn't a problem. By the time she made this decision she was a storehouse of knowledge on the what, why, and how of the vegan lifestyle. Her passion led her to publish a vegan newsletter that included her own original writing, such as this piece:

A Vegan Halloween

Although my trick-or-treating days were cut short when I became a vegan, I still have fabulous Halloweens. I invite all of my best friends to a party where we tramp about in our costumes, play all kinds of games, watch some terrifying movie and make ourselves entirely sick on great quantities of vegan chocolate.

Yes, vegans really can have thoroughly enjoyable Halloweens. For the trick-or-treaters who come to your house, you can buy vegan candy such as Sunspire's Halloween chocolate balls, Barat's chocolate bars (which are small enough for trick-or-treaters) or yummy crisps and chews of any kind. Stickers, pencils and other inexpensive toys are also very appropriate. And even though some of these items are more expensive than un-vegan candy, I believe that it's worth paying a little extra to avoid promoting a cruel industry.

Have a Happy Halloween!

From Rebecca Fletcher, editor

For others, finding the right topic requires a bit more work. Nathan's class was just getting ready to begin report writing. His teacher talked to the class about choosing topics. I watched and could see Nathan sitting slumped in the back, fiddling with his thumbs. Later, he stayed behind as the other children left for their desks.

"You don't look too excited," I said, pulling myself up beside him.

"I hate writing reports," he muttered.

"Yeah. It can be pretty tough," I agreed. I remembered back to my school days and the challenge of trying to squeeze a few more facts out of a book so I could stretch my writing to the end of the page.

"The thing is, Nathan, if you can find just the right topic, it changes the whole thing from something dreary to something exciting." Nathan looked up at me somewhat skeptically, but I took his look as an invitation to continue.

"This could be a time to learn about something that really interests you. What gets you excited?"

"I found a baby snapping turtle yesterday in my front yard. It was all dirty so my dad and me cleaned it off in a bucket of water, and then we walked down to the pond at the end of our street to let it go." As Nathan told this story I sensed his excitement.

"Well, what if you could spend these next couple of weeks finding out more about that snapping turtle? You might be able to figure out how it got in your front yard or what it might have been doing there. And what about what it's doing now? What do you think will happen to that turtle now that it's in the pond?"

Nathan was listening and I was listening, too. I watched his body for signs of enthusiasm. It was important for him to be eager about the topic, not just content to please me. "What do you think?" I asked. "Does this topic really, truly interest you? If so, the research will feel like fun. If not, well, it just might be the kind of report writing that you know you don't like to do."

Nathan considered the difference a topic can make, and by the time we finished talking he was ready to go in search of some books. I also suggested he bring his research into his front yard and spend time investigating for further evidence.

The best nonfiction writing begins with a writer's passionate curiosity about a subject. It's pretty hard to stay interested in the research process if you aren't interested in the topic. We believe that letting students choose their own topics makes a difference in the quality of their nonfiction work.

Use Exploratory Writing to Develop Expertise

Mary Kay Healy uses the term "dump truck writing" to describe students' nonfiction writing. Writers scoop up a truckload of facts from other published sources and then dump them into their drafts. Their own writing becomes but a shadow of the texts they have read before. The writing lacks voice, offering instead a sketchy retelling of what other researchers have come to say about the subject. The art of nonfiction writing lies in the individual way writers shape and convey their understanding of the subject at hand. Readers want evidence of the writer's fingerprints left behind. They want to know they are in the hands of a trusted authority. The second grader whose writing is shown below is still developing his skills, but he clearly understands the harsh realities of Civil War battles, and he has something to say about them!

Early in the process we want students to delay the urge to write a finished report and instead focus on becoming an expert in the subject. Later, once they are walking resources on their topics, they can turn their attention toward writing about them.

What does this mean for the workshop? Early on, students should use writing as a means rather than an end. Zinsser calls this exploratory writing. It includes freewriting about the topic to uncover what you know, jotting a list of the questions you have, capturing phrases or images that seem significant to your understanding of the subject, and freewriting again to explore what you are learning. Exploratory writing happens in and around other processes that go hand in hand: reading, interviewing, observing, and reflecting on their subjects. Students use exploratory writing to learn and to become experts on their subjects. In each of the grade level sections to follow you will find a handful of lessons aimed at the exploratory stage of research writing.

Spend Time Considering What You Already Know

More often than not, the writer already knows something about the subject. Krista wants to write about bats because her class has been building bat houses in science. Andrew's father lets him ride on the tractor while he seeds the field. He has watched his father plant and harvest this field and seen how the tractor makes his father's job easier. Joseph spent Saturday taking apart an old computer, and now he wonders even more how the darn thing works!

Students need to first uncover the experiential knowledge they already possess. Kyle was researching skunks. When asked if he knew anything about them, he answered, "No, but once a skunk got into the garage and messed up our garbage." He knows skunks eat people's garbage, and his father's reaction taught him that some people find them a nuisance. Encourage students to spend time exploring what they already know. Students might do this using a K-W-L strategy (What do you already *k*now? What do you *w*ant to learn? What have you *l*earned?) or they might ask a classmate to interview them about the topic. New questions naturally lead from this experience, and you should encourage students to generate and record these questions for future study. Kyle might now wonder: Do skunks eat only garbage? Why don't people just shoo them away with a stick? Do they come around only at night?

Gather a Wide Range of Resources

Don Murray, Pulitzer Prize–winning nonfiction writer, suggests writers tap three kinds of resources: people, institutions and agencies, and books. Early in my fourth graders' study on colonial New Hampshire I sent a letter home to parents asking if anyone had information to share.

Perhaps you have expertise about a certain aspect of colonial life. Maybe you are a collector and have artifacts that we could look at: clothing, maps, tools, or cookware. Or maybe you know someone who does who would be willing to share with us.

In our midst we had a carpenter who built furniture using colonial tools and methods, and a woman who knew the colonists' art of calligraphy. There were clothes to look at, and one older gentleman came to talk with us about his experience going to school in a one-room schoolhouse.

Together we gathered boxes of books about the general topic from our school library, and I added them to the ones I had found at the local library. There were easy-to-read picture books as well as more challenging history books. (If I were doing this today there would be other "print" resources found on Web pages and CD-ROMs.) At the local historical society we found artists' renderings and personal accounts that helped us get closer to understanding the earliest days of our state's history.

Whether you are embarking on a whole-class study or individual explorations, it's important to let others know what students are studying. One teacher we know posts outside the classroom a list of topics her students are researching and invites people to contact her if they have resources they're willing to share.

By collecting a range of resources we help students build a ladder to help them climb higher and deeper into the subject. Although many students head first to the encyclopedia, encourage them to begin with simple texts. This way students build prior knowledge that they can bring to successively more challenging texts.

Photos or paintings offer opportunities to build knowledge about a topic and can help a student prepare for an interview or generate questions for further research. People, institutions and agencies, and books: Each set of resources enhances the effectiveness of the others.

Familiarize Students with the Particulars of Nonfiction Texts

Nonfiction books are different from the picture storybooks and novels that students more frequently read. Not only does the structure of expository text differ from narrative, but also the format of the book offers support for the nonlinear way a student researcher might approach the book. Share with students how to scan a text to learn what it has to offer. Reading the table of contents along with the introduction usually gives a reader enough information to know what the book is about. Learning to use an index allows students to read purposely for the questions they seek to answer. Students benefit from lessons on how to use subtitles, picture captions, glossaries, charts, and graphs.

Organize Your Note Taking

There are lots of ways to organize information as it's coming in, such as learning logs or journals, index cards, and research folders. It matters less what system you use than that a system exists. Because students will do a variety of writing as they research, it's important for them to have a place to gather that work. Folders work well for me because they allow slips of paper to be ordered and reordered, clipped when they belong together, held side by side. But whether you use folders, learning logs, or something else altogether, your students will probably generate and organize some of the following:

- An ongoing list of questions that arise as they learn more about their topic.

- Notes organized around individual questions. (Some students list one question per page and then use these sheets for collecting notes.)

- A glossary for content-specific words they are learning.

- Early attempts at transforming notes into longer chunks of text. This could be flash drafts (see section 5–8) or simple freewriting. I asked my students to follow every session of note taking with ten minutes of freewriting on what they learned that day about their topic. (No notes allowed while writing!) This helped them bring their own voice to the material. It also pointed out where their knowledge was fuzzy, helping them organize the next day's research.

- A list of resources being used.

Organizing data on paper helps students develop the mental organization they need to make cognitive sense of what they are learning.

Talk About Your Subject to Everyone You Know

Talk, like exploratory writing, helps students get familiar with new information. During all the reading, note taking, and writing, I encourage students to talk, talk, and talk some more. "Teach me what you learned today," I say in a conference. "Come to the author's chair and teach us what you are learning." When students sit before peers and talk about their subjects, they are rehearsing for the day they will write. The talk makes them think about organization. "Where should I start? How can I say this so they'll understand?" When we ask questions based on what they share, it helps students discover what they know and what they need to know.

Write from Abundance

How do you know when you're ready to write? Simple: when you feel ready to teach. At some point, students shift from exploratory writing to writing for presentation. Because the focus has been on becoming an expert, students can often judge when they are expert enough to teach others about their topics. This threshold varies for students at different ages. Of course, research doesn't *only* precede writing. In reality research begets writing, and writing begets more research. And all that research and exploratory writing should result in a storehouse full of information from which students draw as they make the shift into writing for presentation.

Writing well requires selecting the salient facts out of a larger pool. Beginning nonfiction writers will often write all of what they know in their attempts to fill a page or two. Ideally, we want students to have pages of notes and heads full of knowledge that they can cull from, and craft a piece that will both teach and entertain their readers.

Where do literary models fit into all of this? Certainly we need to familiarize students with high-quality nonfiction writing. They need to know the landscape of nonfiction texts so they can navigate that world as they are researching and writing. But first let's familiarize ourselves. In the next chapter we take a brief look at what's available for students in the world of children's nonfiction literature.

Adorning the Table: Nonfiction Literature for Students

I (JoAnn) can still picture the library I visited as a child. The nonfiction section seemed tucked away in a corner, far from the storybook aisles I browsed. But I ventured over because the top of those bookcases was lined with a row of stuffed dead birds. There was a huge barn owl along with an assortment of smaller owls. There were other birds, too. I would stand head to head, looking into the small black bead of an eye. At such close range I could study the feather patterns of color that go unnoticed when you see a bird in the wild. I loved to visit the nonfiction aisle.

But none of the books nestled in the cases below had the same appeal of those preserved objects of nature, not with their large blocks of text and far too few black and white drawings sprinkled on the pages. A title promised *The Wonderful World of Science,* but inside there appeared no world of wonder. Just dry, boring text.

How things have changed! The field of children's literature has blossomed and flourished in the last four decades. This is true across the board in the novels, poetry, and picture books available for children of all ages. But none of the changes seem quite as dramatic as those seen in nonfiction titles, most notably in the catalog of informational picture books that has grown to cover nearly every topic a young child might wonder about.

Surely not all nonfiction writing is found between the covers of books.

Magazines, newspapers, brochures, and pamphlets all offer models students can learn from. Like many children in classrooms today, our youngest son reads the *Scholastic News* that comes to his class each week. His teacher can easily tap that resource to help her first and second graders learn about nonfiction writing.

Nonfiction shows up everywhere and in lots of different forms. If students are alive to the possibilities, their options will be broader when it comes time to write. Although students will sometimes choose to write the standard report, they may decide that a threefold brochure or a newsletter, copied and circulated, better suits their purposes.

Even within the informational picture books that flood our school libraries, you will find a range not only of topics, but also of genre and presentation styles. Here's a short tour of subgenres found within the format of informational picture books. You'll want to take your students on a similar tour as they consider how best to write about their subjects.

Concept Books

Many young children are first introduced to nonfiction writing through concept books. We know them as the chunky board books that explore the colors of the rainbow or present one shape on each three-dimensional page. Our classroom libraries are full of concept books as well. Concept books attempt to describe a single object or class of objects, or an abstract idea, in language that helps the reader develop an understanding of the new concept. *Is a Blue Whale the Biggest Thing There Is?* (Robert E. Wells) explores the concept of "large." How big is big? Wells helps readers imagine unfathomable sizes—the universe, or the number one million—by beginning with what the reader already knows. (Counting to a million would take steady counting ten hours a day for about three weeks.) This kind of writing fits naturally with young writers who want to write an all-about book.

Older students can learn from concept books as well. *My Map Book* (Sara Fanelli) includes labeled maps of the narrator's bedroom, a map of her day, and a map of her heart, in its attempt to help youngsters understand the concept of mapping. This book stretches the concept by offering pictorial representations not only of space but also of time and emotions, making it suitable for older as well as younger readers.

Talking Walls: The Story Continues (Margy Burns Knight) explores the concept of diverse cultures by showing us walls from around the world. Knight focuses on the stories walls tell about the people who have constructed or taken them down. Her trip around the globe highlights the way in which various cultures are both similar to and different from one another. In our students' writing we may think of this as thematic focus. When students choose to write all about a central idea, and show it in its many different facets and forms, their expository writing fits the form found in concept books.

Grand Tour (or Survey) Books

Some books attempt to introduce readers to a substantial topic by providing an overall view of it. Writers include a selection of facts and principles in their quest to provide a broad, rather than deep, view of the topic. Anne Rockwell's *Our Earth* does this for primary students. Rockwell gives us a grand tour of the earth by starting in a neighborhood where we might live and taking us to the North Pole, through canyons and deserts, and back to our neighborhood. On this tour she shows young readers how changes in the earth's surfaces occur. We learn how islands are formed and lakes and oceans are filled. For much older readers, *A Drop of Water: A Book of Science and Wonder* (Walter Wick) offers an intriguing survey of water and its properties. Today's information books aren't afraid to blend genres. Wick's book ends with another subgenre—activity and experimentation writing—when he offers three pages of observations and experiments readers can try on their own.

Specialized Books

In contrast to the grand tour book we find the texts that focus on specific information about a specialized subject. These books focus on a relatively limited topic, and are well suited to the writer who brings a passion and deep knowledge of a narrow topic. A boy owns two Great Danes and understands the specifics of this animal—what they eat, how they are trained, their temperament, and the particular challenges of living with dogs the size of small ponies. Once this boy gathers research to accompany his experiential knowledge, he can write well about a specialized subject. He might learn from Eve Bunting's book *The Wall* how a story can teach us about a specialized topic. Or he can draw on the model Jennifer Owings Dewey presents in *Poison Dart Frogs.* This text will show him the range of information he might include to give his readers a deep understanding of his subject.

Sometimes a writer will select a particular angle of a larger topic and craft an intriguing specialized report. In *Eating the Plates: A Pilgrim Book of Food and Manners,* Lucille Recht Penner leaves out much about colonial life and dedicates her attention solely to the eating habits, customs, and manners of the Pilgrims. The specialized topic asks for depth rather than breadth, making it an appropriate challenge for students who are ready.

Life Cycle Books

Students seem to have an endless fascination with animals and other aspects of life around them. Life cycle books explore the growth and change of living elements. They may choose to focus on all or part of the life cycle. *Jack's*

Garden (Henry Cole) shows us one boy's garden from seed to harvest, filling the frame of each page with labeled drawings of the many earthly elements that interact with it. *Pond Year* (Kathryn Lasky) reveals the fertile life of a pond and the changes it undergoes from one spring to the next. Each of these titles, like all life cycle books, use time as an organizing element.

When a student's topic explores all or part of a life cycle, it's helpful for her to see how authors of other life cycle books or essays use the inherent element of time to organize their writing. Whereas some writers rely on the straightforward order of events, others such as Bruce Hiscock in *The Big Tree* may choose to present their subject as it stands today and then jump back in time to pick up the thread of the story of its growth.

Biography

Although students may research from larger texts, picture book biographies provide students with texts that model the size and scope of the biographies they'll attempt to write. In books such as *Snowflake Bentley* by Jacqueline Briggs Martin and Peter Sis's *Starry Messenger: A Book Depicting the Life of a Famous Scientist, Mathematician, Astronomer, Philosopher, Physicist, Galileo Galilei* you'll find the traditional biographical form in which the author presents the subject's life beginning with birth and ending with death. For some students, partial biography offers a more useful model. *Wilma Unlimited* (Kathleen Krull), *America's Champion Swimmer: Gertrude Ederle* (David A. Adler), and *The Microscope* (Maxine Kumin) all focus on a slice of time in the lives of their subjects. This form can help students avoid a superficial survey of a person's life, and lead them to detail significant accomplishments with more richly textured prose.

Some biographers highlight a theme and then weave information about historical figures into the story of a particular event. In *Teammates* (Peter Golenbock) we consider personal courage in the face of racial prejudice and learn about Jackie Robinson and Pee Wee Reese. The pioneer courage of early suffragettes in *Bloomers* (Rhoda Blumberg) becomes the backdrop of an introduction to Susan B. Anthony, Amelia Bloomer, and Elizabeth Cady Stanton.

These books display a range of presentation styles. You can read compelling stories: in one case, a poem. Some authors use the space on the page to tuck odd facts outside the text. Sis gives us Galileo's own words in quotes that appear to be hand scripted. In *Snowflake Bentley* frames set along the left and right edges of the page hold interesting details ("Starting at age fifteen he drew a hundred snow crystals each winter for three winters"). These books are playful and informative. Help your students discover the way writers are portraying historical figures, and invite them to be playful with their own biographical writing.

And then there are others: photographic essays, documents and journals, craft and how-to books, and identification books. Readers who journey into children's nonfiction will find a rich and varied landscape. You might begin by reading aloud choice books. Then ask your students, What kind of writing do we have here? Or you may ask children to generate all the kinds of nonfiction writing they notice in the world and invite them to search for examples that show it being done well.

Finally, don't make the mistake of discounting those books that strike you first as storybooks. Many of them blur the edges between narrative and expository writing by providing wonderful examples of short, snappy nonfiction in the end materials found outside the narrative frame of the story. Some of our favorite nonfiction shorts are found in the backs of the following books: Denise Fleming's *Where Once There Was a Wood* (How to Build a Backyard Habitat for Birds), Lois Ehlert's *Feathers for Lunch* (the lunch that got away: a field guide of birds), and Lynn Cherry's *The Armadillo from Amarillo* (in which the author's note offers a delightful physical description of an armadillo along with clarification of separating fact from fiction in the preceding story). Read. Revel. Reveal. And enjoy!

Lesson Craft

FEATURED TITLES

Nonfiction Craft Lessons K–2

*W*alk into a primary classroom during writing workshop and you might find two girls working on an alphabet book, a boy writing about his birthday, another boy writing about going fishing with his uncle, a girl writing a fairy tale, and two boys working on a scary story. But chances are good that you will also find a boy writing about sharks, a girl writing about elephants, and so forth.

The primary years are a period of intense learning. Children begin to master enormously complex skills such as reading, writing, and tying their shoes. And they have a real hunger to learn more about the world. The real world of vipers, crystals, dinosaurs, and quicksand mesmerizes kids at this age. They read nonfiction books at the library, and it's no surprise when they want to write in this genre, too. We need to create classrooms in which they can learn more about the subjects that interest them, and can write about them in a way that is appropriate to their age level.

At the end of first grade, our son Joseph remarked while we were driving in the car, "I want to do lots of research about monkeys and apes."

I was struck by the seriousness of his tone. At the same time I was aware that Joseph was very much of an emergent writer. He faced a huge mismatch between his ambitions and what he could actually do in terms of research and writing. That's pretty typical. Primary children have all the passion and fascination that older kids have. But we should be realistic about what these students can and cannot do when they pick up their pencils and markers.

What does nonfiction writing look like at this age level? For one thing, much of the information gets embedded in detailed pictures these children draw. It's important not to dismiss their importance. Drawings give children the opportunity to create their own symbols to make sense of the world. When we confer with them, we can show real interest in these drawings and ask questions about the visual details. You will notice that this section includes several craft lessons pertaining to students' drawings.

Children at this age often do not distinguish nonfiction writing from narrative writing. Instead, we typically see a blend of "story information writing" not unlike some of the nonfiction children's literature available. For example Darlene, a first grader, wrote this piece:

> We heard some birds. When we looked into a tree we saw a bird's nest! Dad lifted me up on his shoulders so I could peek inside. When he did I saw three eggs. They were turquoise blue. Dad said they were robins' eggs. I can't wait till they hatch and we have baby robins.

This is a first-person narrative in which Darlene has woven certain facts about robins: the nest and the color of the eggs. Teachers who work with older children work to erase the "I" from their work, but at this level, at least, we should encourage kids to include themselves in the writing. In this way, they can write with voice, and they can connect what they are learning to their own lives.

You'll notice that this section begins with a handful of exploratory craft lessons. Here we suggest ways these children can use talking, writing, and drawing to think their way into a deeper understanding of their subjects.

Nonfiction literature geared to children of this age includes many different formats. Given the mismatch between students' interests and their abilities, teachers might nourish nonfiction writers on two kinds of books. We can share with them books such as *I Want to Be an Astronaut* by Byron Barton, a simple text that has a picture and a single sentence on each page. A book such as this one gives young children an image of what their own teaching books might look like. At the same time, we should give them plenty of access to more complex books (the Eyewitness Series, for example) that will be great for their own research, even if the writing is beyond what most kids can do at that age.

The guiding principles for working with our youngest nonfiction writers are three Ps: passion, play, and patience (ours). Most primary-age children are not ready to learn the nuts and bolts of reports. There will be plenty of time for them to learn the particulars of paragraphing, footnotes, and the like. Many of the craft lessons you'll find in this section suggest simple formats that will allow primary-level children to present their learnings in a way that doesn't overwhelm them or turn them off. We should look at research and nonfiction writing as our chance to extend their deep wonder and curiosity about the world in which we live.

Exploratory: Observing the World

RESOURCE MATERIAL

❧ *If You Find a Rock* by Peggy Christian

❧ *One Small Square* by Donald M. Silver

❧ Small blank notebooks

DISCUSSION

Young children have a natural curiosity about the natural world. We should tap into that curiosity as we introduce them to information writing. Researching involves more than simply copying facts out of a book. It is being alive to the world, and valuing one's perceptions of the world. In this craft lesson we explore the idea of observation. We want our students to begin to trust and learn from how they experience the physical world. You can encourage careful observation by providing them with some sort of notebook that can be used as a container to hold their perceptions.

HOW TO TEACH IT

Have you ever felt the cottony stuff inside a milkweed pod? Have you ever heard the peepers (frogs) making a racket in the spring? Have you ever smelled a skunk cabbage, or a skunk?

When you did that, you were paying close attention to the world. That's called *observation*. Scientists are trained to observe the world, whether it's a one-celled amoeba or immense galaxies. You observe the world by looking very carefully. And when you observe, you also use your other four senses—smell, sound, touch, and taste.

We've been reading some books that talk about how important it is to observe the world. Remember this book *If You Find a Rock*? The author talks about all the things you can do if you find a special rock.

Another book, *One Small Square,* shows you all the things you can see just from closely studying one small piece of your backyard.

(Go to page 9 of *One Small Square.*)

This book has ideas about how you might keep a backyard notebook where you can write down what you notice. I've put together some blank notebooks you could use. In this notebook you can draw pictures and write words to explain what you saw. Before you write or draw a picture in your notebook, it's important to take a really good look so you can mark down as many details as possible. When you do that, you're really living like a scientist.

Exploratory: Talking Before You Write

RESOURCE MATERIAL

🐾 Books that provide historical photos

🐾 *One More River to Cross: An African American Photograph Album* by Walter Dean Myers

🐾 *Kids at Work: Lewis Hine and the Crusade Against Child Labor* by Russell Freedman

🐾 *Century Farm: One Hundred Years on a Family Farm* by Cris Peterson

DISCUSSION

Lisa Siemens teaches primary children in Winnipeg, Canada. As you read this, notice how carefully she structures her students' talk.

HOW TO TEACH IT

"As a young girl I became fascinated by old news, not so much through reading the printed word, but more through studying the grainy old photos—children dressed in high boots and bonnets, etc. I wanted to get inside those pictures. Now when my students study the past, I go right back to my early fascination with images. I make overheads of historical pictures, choosing photographs that relate to particular issues, photographs that might open the door to deep conversations.

"When we first begin class discussions of this kind, I ask five or six students to form a circle within our larger circle. They look at the overhead picture and begin talking—describing what they see, asking questions, hypothesizing, relating things they think they know to the picture before them, agreeing, disagreeing—and the rest of us listen in.

"At the end of the conversation, after about five or ten minutes, the inner-circle children discuss how their 'talk' went—whether they were listening to each other, whether they invited others into the conversations, the kinds of comments or questions that opened up conversation or brought it to a standstill. Then the outer-circle observers tell them what they noticed. I have found this to be one of the best ways of preparing children to go off into small groups or carry on their own conversations. Over a number of days the children meet in small groups to discuss a variety of pictures. Then, after lots of talk and some clarification on points of confusion, they choose one of the pictures to write extensively about.

"For example, it wasn't until the children saw the photograph of a Cree family standing outside their teepee that they realized that European settlers were not the 'first people' here at all. Chloe and Erinn wrote about this photo:

> When the settlers first came to Manitoba, many Cree people and other tribes still lived a nomadic life, but many died of the diseases settlers brought from the old country. Before the settlers came, the tribes would move with the food, but when the settlers came, they said you live here and don't move, because we get all that land. We can't believe that they were so unfair."

Exploratory: Taking Notes

RESOURCE MATERIAL

❧ Paper folded into fourths

DISCUSSION

The question we must ask in working with young nonfiction writers is, How can we challenge them without overwhelming them with unrealistic expectations? Good teachers get a sense of how far their students can go. And this is important if we want to introduce them to the many subskills involved in this kind of writing. Certain concepts in content-area writing—note taking, leads, conclusions—can be introduced in a way so that even our youngest can get a feel for what it means to take a crash course on a subject and create their own teaching books.

The following craft lesson shows one way of helping students pull facts from a trade book. Although there should be other kinds of note taking, the skills described here will prove important throughout students' years in school.

HOW TO TEACH IT

JoAnn Wong-Kam teaches in Honolulu. Here she describes a simple note-taking strategy that has proven to be manageable with her second-grade students.

"The K-W-L strategy is one that I sometimes use. (What do you *k*now about your topic? What do you *w*ant to learn? What have you *l*earned?) But with the younger students sometimes this is too broad and doesn't offer them enough support. So I have them take a piece of paper and fold it into fourths.

"Then, as they look through trade books, I ask them to write down something that interests them about their topic. They can draw a simple picture with a caption in their space. But the space is small enough so they don't try to copy too much information from the book.

"After they complete two to three papers (eight to twelve notes) we cut the facts apart and they try to organize them. They decide what should come first, what facts maybe go together. They look to see if there are more things they want to add, or specific things they want to put in. They do this fact review with the teacher or peers. After a few more facts are collected and added to the organized collection, the students begin writing their drafts. These are made into mini-books and shared at author's chair. This has worked well with my second graders because it gives them an understanding of the process of research, and it's not too formal."

Exploratory: Collecting "Dash Facts" on a Topic

RESOURCE MATERIAL

🔊 Unlined paper folded into fourths, or divided into four boxes (Appendix A)

DISCUSSION

Our son Joseph said, "I think I want to research all about monkeys and apes." We wanted to build his curiosity, and wondered how we could best take advantage of it. Joseph was in first grade. Teachers who work with primary writers face a mismatch between students' passion and what they can realistically do. Here's a simple method you can use to help students begin pulling factual information from nonfiction texts. For this craft lesson we are indebted to Joseph's teacher, Jane Winsor, who teaches a multiage first/second grade classroom in New Hampshire.

HOW TO TEACH IT

"Last year our first graders worked on a class book about the planets," Jane says. "I wanted them to do some simple research, and I wanted to do it in a way that wouldn't overwhelm them. As they did their research, I had them write facts onto the paper. We call these *dash facts*. I asked them to write a dash at the beginning of each fact they gathered. And I modeled for them how they could write it quickly, just getting the information down, without having to use complete sentences. Later, after each student had gathered a number of dash facts, I (plus a few parent volunteers) helped the kids put the facts into complete sentences for the book.

"This year the kids are going to research bears. I'll have the kids fold a piece of paper into fourths. One quarter of the paper might be used for collecting dash facts about the food bears eat. Another quarter might be used for collecting dash facts about habitat, etc. In that way, folding the paper helps the kids organize the dash facts they collect."

Once you have shared this strategy with students, you can encourage them to use it while researching their own topics by providing them with paper divided into fourths.

Exploratory: Taking Notes from an Illustration

RESOURCE MATERIAL

🕭 *Amazing Snakes* by Alexandra Parsons

🕭 Post-it notes

DISCUSSION

A picture is worth a thousand words. Watch children read an information book, and you'll notice that their eyes are drawn first to the photographs or drawings. When students study photographs or detailed pictures, they learn more about their topics. They also discover the important role pictures play in nonfiction texts, making it more likely that they will use teaching illustrations in their own writing.

HOW TO TEACH IT

Have you ever had a hard time explaining something to someone and found yourself wishing you had a picture to show them instead? That's because a picture can show you what something looks like or how it works. In the same way, writers use pictures in their books to teach us about their subjects. When we really study a picture, we can learn a lot. Taking notes helps you learn more from the pictures or photographs in the books you are reading.

Let me show you what that looks like. (Select any of the Eyewitness Junior Books. In this lesson, we refer to the page "The Deadly Cobra" in *Amazing Snakes*.)

Let's take a look at this page in the Eyewitness Book *Amazing Snakes*. The authors use photographs and drawings as well as words to teach us about the cobra. (As you look together at this page, encourage the students to talk about what they are learning from the pictures.) Let's use Post-it notes to jot down what the pictures are teaching us. I'm going to write, "Cobras hatch from eggs" and put it next to this illustration. What's something one of you learned from the pictures? (As students share their ideas, write each on a Post-it note and stick it on the picture on the page.)

Today when you are researching, try taking notes from the pictures the author has included. When you are finished with the book, you can take off the Post-its and place them in your research notebook. These notes will help when it comes time to write your own teaching book.

(At a later date you might want to show students how they can organize and reorganize the facts once they are in their notebooks.)

Exploratory: Talking About Your Research

RESOURCE MATERIAL

▪ None

DISCUSSION

James Britton once said that in a classroom "reading and writing float on a sea of talk." Talk helps students discover what they know and what they need to know next. It helps them integrate what they are learning into their own understandings. We've placed this exploratory lesson in the K–2 section because it's simple enough for the youngest child to do. However, the process of talking about your growing expertise is a valuable and, we think, essential strategy for writers of all ages.

HOW TO TEACH IT

The best way to really understand what you're learning is to teach someone else. We're going to be using our author's chair a little differently as we continue our research. Each day, I'll invite two or three of you to come sit in the author's chair. Your task will be to teach us about what you are learning. The rest of us will listen and learn. We'll ask questions about any part we want to hear more about or those places we don't understand. Our questions will help you consider if and where you need to do more research.

   (In general it is best to ask students to talk without notes so they are relying on their own words in discussing the topic. We recommend you take notes for each student who shares. You might list any questions the student can't answer but feels are important. Or you might record places where the student seems confused about information. These notes can focus the student's research efforts for the next day.)

Exploratory: Listening for Your Voice

RESOURCE MATERIAL

❧ List of factual statements written on chart paper. We suggest you create your own based on the specific topics your students are writing about.

DISCUSSION

Listen to children when they are in the throes of animated conversation. They have the most wonderfully inventive ways of saying things. Yet when it comes time to write nonfiction, they often put aside their speaking voices for a more formal and less interesting voice. Martha Horn often invites students to talk about their subjects before writing. She listens and, in turn, helps students hear the potential voices they bring to their own writing.

HOW TO TEACH IT

Before we head to writing today, I'm going to ask you to partner up with someone and to each spend five minutes talking about your subject. During this time I want you to share with them anything you want about your topic. Talk about what you find most interesting or surprising. Your partner will listen and maybe ask questions to encourage you to talk more.

Find a partner and decide who will talk first. I'll let you know when it's time to switch.

(While students are talking, listen in and selectively take verbatim notes so you can later share with the students the words they are using to describe their topics. You might want to jot them on a chart to later compare with other factual statements that represent the kind of dry, factual writing students might be tempted to use.)

Let's take a look at this chart and listen to the language you used to talk about your topics. (Read the list of selective student comments and then the list of dry, factual statements.) Both of these give facts about a subject. Which would you rather listen to? Which would be more interesting for a reader? When you write today, try writing about your facts in the same kind of voice you might use if you were talking to a friend.

Copyright © 2001

JoAnn Portalupi and

Ralph Fletcher.

Stenhouse Publishers

Using a Draft Book to Lay Out Information

RESOURCE MATERIAL

⁂ Blank draft books

⁂ Post-it notes

DISCUSSION

The draft book can help young writers organize the factual material they dig up. These books are easy to make: staple together six to eight half sheets of unlined paper. Ask students to write on one side of the page only when working on early drafts. The format makes it easy to cluster related facts on the same page. Although young writers aren't yet thinking about paragraphs, this lays the groundwork for them to pick up this skill in the future.

HOW TO TEACH IT

Sometimes it's helpful to imagine your topic as a finished book before you even start writing. You can use a draft book to help you do this. This is what it looks like. A draft book is a place to write just like a sheet of paper except you have many pages. These pages help you collect information that belongs together, and separate what doesn't. If I were writing an information book about our school, I might sit with my empty draft book and imagine what it could look like when it's all finished.

(Model this for students by turning page by page and talking aloud about what information you might put on each page.)

Maybe I'll begin with people who come to school and the different jobs they have. Next, I'll talk about different rooms in the school. Then I'll talk about school rules. There could be a page on what's outside the building—the playground! At the end I want a page for special facts about our school, such as where the name came from and when it was built.

As I'm planning this out, I'm going to write down one or two words on a Post-it note and stick it to each blank page of my draft book. These Post-it notes will help me remember what will go on each page when I write my book. When I'm finished with the Post-its I'll have a map to guide me as I write.

If you are ready to begin writing about your topic, you might try using a draft book to imagine how the information will be organized. It might help to talk it through just as I did. If you want to do that, find someone to listen to you. Don't forget to jot notes on the Post-its so you will have a map to follow as you get going.

Writing a Table of Contents

RESOURCE MATERIAL

🐟 *Whales* by Deborah Hodge

🐟 Easel with chart paper

DISCUSSION

The *last* thing we want to do is overwhelm young writers. When we push a student to master a skill that is beyond his comfort zone, we create anxiety that can stop the child's writing development cold.

With that caution in mind, we should recognize that primary children have a natural fascination with some of the sophisticated features of books—the dedication, appendix, copyright page, and so forth. The following craft lesson builds on this curiosity. Having students create a simple table of contents will help them organize their informational writing. We believe that this craft lesson has tremendous value for 3–4 and 5–8 students, too.

HOW TO TEACH IT

Have you ever opened the door to a closet where everything is jumbled together so that you can't find what you're looking for? If you take the time to organize things with shelves or boxes—the shoes down here, the sweaters over there—you can find what you need when you need it.

Books are that way, too. Some books have lots of good information, but it's all mixed up and you can't find what you want. Today I'm going to show you one way you can organize your information and solve this problem.

Let's look at this book, *Whales* by Deborah Hodge. We open the book and see the title page. But the second page has this heading: Contents. This is called the table of contents. What do you think this is for? (Discuss.)

A table of contents shows how the information is organized into chapters. If I want to know where whales live, I'll turn to the fourth chapter. If I want to know what whales eat, I'll go to this chapter on page twenty. This author has created "shelves" in her "closet" so readers know exactly where to look for what they want to know.

Let's say you're writing about spiders. What chapters would you have to organize your information? (Discuss. Write a sample table of contents on a large chart.)

You could write a table of contents, too. It doesn't have to be longer than three or four chapters. It's a great way to organize what you're writing about, for you and for your readers. If you're interested, take out a piece of paper and try to imagine what sections you will have.

Anticipating Readers' Questions

RESOURCE MATERIAL

❦ None

DISCUSSION

We tell young writers, Imagine what information your readers will need so they can picture your story. This advice pertains to narrative, but it is even more important in content-area writing. Anticipating questions that a reader might have requires a cognitive leap that some me-centered primary children are not ready to make. Even so, it's important to air this issue with them.

HOW TO TEACH IT

Sometimes we have a burning question: Why don't puppies open their eyes when they are born? or What causes a tidal wave? We read books to find answers to those questions. When you write an information book, you need to give your readers answers to their questions about what you are writing about.

In one classroom, a boy named Ross wanted to write a teaching book about how you get honey from a beehive. He had learned about this because his grandfather had beehives on his farm. Before he started writing his teaching book, he sat in the author's chair and told the other kids what he was going to write about. As you might imagine, the kids had tons of questions:

Were the bees noisy? Was it dangerous?
What did you wear so you wouldn't get stung?
Did the stuff in the hive look different from regular honey?

Later, when Ross wrote his teaching book, he remembered the questions all the kids asked him. In his book, he tried to answer their questions.

(Note to teachers: It is probably even more effective to use a similar example from one of your own students who shared his or her area of expertise with classmates.)

Many of you are writing teaching books. As you write, try to imagine that you sitting in the author's chair, answering questions about what you are writing about. What questions would other kids have?

It might even help to get together with one person and ask your partner to help you brainstorm questions readers might have about your topic.

Labeling a Picture

RESOURCE MATERIAL

🐾 *Feathers for Lunch* by Lois Ehlert

🐾 *The Honey Makers* by Gail Gibbons

🐾 *Sea Turtles* by Gail Gibbons

DISCUSSION

Young writers go through a developmental process in which the way they express themselves moves gradually from pictures to words. One of the earliest forms of alphabetic writing occurs when they begin to label their pictures. This kind of simple labeling may look quite primitive—FT will stand for "fire truck"—but it marks a significant foray into print. This craft lesson is most applicable to kindergarten, early first grade, or emerging writers.

HOW TO TEACH IT

I've been enjoying your writing. Many of you have drawn detailed pictures that have taught me a lot about what you're writing about.

(Share a few examples of students' picture stories.)

I'd like to show you something interesting. I've brought in a couple of teaching books: *Feathers for Lunch* by Lois Ehlert, plus these books about bees and sea turtles. In *Feathers for Lunch* you'll notice this picture of a bird, and right here there's a word that tells the name of this bird: robin. That is called a label.

(Show examples from other books.)

You notice that when these illustrators label their pictures, they don't write the word on the top of the page. Instead, they write the word right next to what they drew.

When you draw a picture, it's a good idea to label the drawing so the reader will understand what it is. Today I'd like to encourage you to label some of the important things you want us to know about. Let's say you've got a picture of a woman in a garden with a squiggly thing on the ground. Is it a snake? Is it a worm? We won't know unless you label the drawing.

Making a Diagram

RESOURCE MATERIAL

❧ *Bugs* by Nancy Winslow Parker and Joan Richards Wright

❧ *My Map Book* by Sara Fanelli

❧ Any other book with diagrams

DISCUSSION

In the previous craft lesson, we encouraged students to teach the reader by making a drawing and labeling it. This lesson on how to make a diagram builds on that one. We initially combined these lessons, but the number of subskills involved convinced us they needed to be separate. Because a diagram leans heavily on the drawing and requires a minimum number of words, this craft lesson is a good fit for emerging writers.

HOW TO TEACH IT

Today I want us to take a close look at a book we have read before: *Bugs.* You might remember that in this book the authors wrote about each different bug in a particular way. They wrote a rhyming riddle, they drew a diagram, and then they gave more detailed information. A diagram is a sketch or drawing that explains a thing by showing all its different parts. Let's take a good look at some of these diagrams. What do you notice?

(Show diagrams. Briefly discuss with class.)

When you make a diagram you give the reader a detailed picture of your subject. Let's try this together. Let's suppose we're writing about trees. Okay, so let's start with a drawing:

(Sketch a tree on an easel. You might want to have done this ahead of time. The sketch should be detailed enough to include roots, bark, the trunk, leaves, bird nests, and leaves.)

Which parts do we need to label?

(Gather ideas from kids, and label the parts of your tree.)

Today when you write you may want to make a diagram to help your readers learn about your subject. Start with your drawing. After you draw it, go back and label the parts. When you are finished, go back and take another look at your diagram. There may be other important parts you left out and need to include.

Drawing a Series of Pictures to Show Change

RESOURCE MATERIAL

❧ Appendixes B1 and B2

DISCUSSION

Many of the topics young children study involve learning how something changes over time. Seeds grow into flowers. Caterpillars turn into butterflies. Creating a series of pictures is a natural way to convey information about growth. Once students understand labeling diagrams, you may want to teach them how to write a series of captioned pictures that show change over time.

HOW TO TEACH IT

Some of you are writing about topics that change over time. For instance, a seed planted in the ground sprouts and then sends up a little shoot that later forms leaves until it grows into a mature plant. You can show these kinds of changes by using a series of drawings. Here's an example of how a writer might teach about a seed sprouting into a flower.

(Share Appendix B1.)

Notice that each picture looks similar. Some part of each picture stays the same: the line of the ground, the tree in the background, the sun in the sky. But one part of each picture has been drawn to show how the seed is changing over time. The writer adds a caption—or a sentence—underneath each picture to help you know what is happening in each new drawing. You can read the words and study the pictures to see how seeds change into flowers.

Does what you're studying about change over time?

(Discuss.)

If so, you might try drawing a series of pictures like this one. I've made a sheet with blank boxes (see Appendix B2). You can use this paper to help you design your pictures and write your captions. Or you may want to make your own boxes. In the next few days I'll ask whoever tries this idea to share your work with us.

Copyright © 2001

JoAnn Portalupi and

Ralph Fletcher.

Stenhouse Publishers

Figuring Out What Is (and Isn't) True

RESOURCE MATERIAL

❧ The Magic School Bus books by Joanna Cole

DISCUSSION

Yes, truth matters in nonfiction writing. Yes, we want to begin steering these young writers toward making their writing in this genre more factually accurate. But this must be done gently. Primary children are famous for their wild imaginations, and the concept of absolute truth can be hard to swallow. Here we introduce the idea so they can begin thinking about it.

HOW TO TEACH IT

When we read fairy tales we expect all sorts of magical things to happen. Humans change into animals, seeds grow into gigantic beanstalks, hens lay golden eggs. When we read information books we read some pretty amazing things, too (for example, some spiders build webs that are twenty-seven feet long!), but we can be pretty sure that the author isn't just making them up. In an information book we expect that what we read will be true. In this case, "true" means that it is the way things are in the real world.

A first-grade girl wrote a teaching book: All About Trees. On page one, she had a picture and information about an apple tree. On page two she wrote about a cherry tree. On page three she wrote about the huge sequoia tree. So far so good. On page seven she wrote about a "leather tree." There were branches with big strips of leather hanging off the tree. Does that sound true? Actually leather is made from the skin of cows. It doesn't grow on trees. On page eight she wrote about a "money tree," a big tree with one-, five-, and ten-dollar bills growing instead of leaves. Is that true? This is funny and clever, but it isn't true. (I wish it were!)

You all know the Magic School Bus books. Lots of wild, zany things happen in these books. At the end of each book the author explains which parts are true and which parts could never really happen. That way readers won't be confused.

When you write your teaching book, you should make sure your facts and details are true. You shouldn't just make things up. It's all right to make a guess at first (that's called a hypothesis), but then you need to do some more research to find out whether or not your guess was right.

Have you written any parts that aren't true? Are there parts where you guessed, or weren't sure? Put a check mark next to those parts. You and I can talk about how you can check further to find out if your information is true.

Writing an Alphabet Information Book

RESOURCE MATERIAL

ᐧᐁ *The Freshwater Alphabet Book* by Jerry Pallotta

DISCUSSION

This craft lesson comes from Lisa Siemens, our colleague in Winnipeg, Canada. An alphabet book is a great model for information writing—both for gathering and for presenting information. But for primary children, writing an alphabet book isn't as easy as it looks. You'll notice that Lisa and her students work together on a class alphabet book about a subject they are all studying. In this way, she gives them a positive common experience they can build on.

HOW TO TEACH IT

"Jerry Pallotta's alphabet books are the most wonderfully accessible books for young readers who want to learn about a wide range of subjects," Lisa says. "They are equally accessible and helpful to young writers. When my students were raising monarch butterflies, eagerly watching them evolve from day to day, completely awestruck, they gathered information from a wide range of sources—through observation, videos, science texts, picture books, even poetry. They created amazing poetry, but also learned from Jerry Pallotta how to write an information book.

"On the wall at the front of our room we had a Monarch Alphabet Wall. As we discovered more and more about monarchs, we added words to our walls—A for antennae, abdomen, and adult. B for butterfly. C for chrysalis, caterpillar, coiled tongue, etc. At the very end of June, while our butterflies were emerging daily, we examined Jerry Pallotta's *The Freshwater Alphabet Book,* noticing how he often asks questions and invites the reader into the world of fish. We each wrote and illustrated our own letter of the alphabet, beginning with 'A is for antennae' and ending with

> Z is for zoom! There goes another Monarch. Wow! That was the fastest one today! It was faster than my dog when he runs. And it was faster than us. Bye! We have to go now. ZOOM!"

Creating a "Description Card" for an Old Object or Artifact

RESOURCE MATERIAL

ⁱ Old objects or historical artifacts from students' homes

DISCUSSION

This craft lesson also comes from our friend Lisa Siemens. Here Lisa explains how she guides her students in writing the kind of "description card" you might find in a museum next to an exhibit—a great way to introduce kids to thinking, talking, and writing about history. This kind of brief writing is a perfect match for primary kids.

HOW TO TEACH IT

"When we study the past, I am always aware of how little well-written expository material has been created for young children," Lisa says. "While there are fictional accounts of pioneer days, finding engaging nonfiction material is more difficult. Because I want the children to feel some ownership of their discoveries, and because I know young children need to actually handle concrete materials, I ask them to begin by bringing their own old objects to school. We create a class museum, complete with description cards to go with each item. When the children bring the items in, they have a chance to tell what they know about their object. Sometimes their parents have told them stories; other times all they know is that it is 'old.' (For some children, 'old' is a dial phone; for others it is an old-fashioned crank phone.)

"The children break into small discussion groups, take one object, talk about it, and wonder about it. Since the intent is for each object to have a description card, we begin our writing in a large group, choosing one of the objects and writing a card together. We talk about writing in a way that will both interest and inform museum visitors. After we write about one or two artifacts together, the children work in pairs, each pair writing about one object. Sarah and Chloe wrote about an old tea set:

> Long ago people were probably more interested in animals, because they painted pictures of cows and goats on these dishes. In the tea pot, there are seven little holes to stop the leaves from going in their cups. We have no clue where the cups for this set are, but maybe at Sarah's great-aunt's house. The china company that made these dishes began in 1794. We don't know exactly how old these dishes are.

"The description cards are typed and laminated and placed in our museum. The last time we did this project, we felt so bad about dismantling our museum that we created a permanent record of our exhibit, compiling a museum album that included illustrations, photographs, and descriptions of our class collection."

Writing Through a Mask

RESOURCE MATERIAL

❧ *Sierra* by Diane Siebert

DISCUSSION

I visited a kindergarten class in which a girl approached, meowing.

"Ha!" I laughed. "Are you pretending you're a cat?"

"I'm not pretending," she said angrily. "I *am* a cat!"

Primary kids love to pretend, dress up, play make-believe. This craft lesson challenges them to use their imagination and actually become the thing they are writing about. It's a great way for them to describe their subject from the inside out. We suggest one book to model this element of craft. We know other books written in the same format—especially *Voices of the Wild* by Jonathan London—but they are out of print. (Check www.powells.com and www.bibliofind.com to find out-of-print books.)

HOW TO TEACH IT

Let's start by looking at *Sierra* by Diane Siebert.

(Read.)

What did you notice about how she writes about the mountains? She writes, "I am the mountain . . ." Of course, Diane Siebert is a woman, not a mountain, but in this book she pretends to be the thing she is writing about.

This is a great way to write about what you have been learning about. Let's say you're writing about a sequoia tree. You would start by imagining what it would be like to be that giant tree, the largest living thing on this planet. You have to pretend that you are a sequoia and talk about yourself to the reader. This is called "writing through a mask." You put on the mask of your subject and become that thing. You could do the same thing for almost any subject—a volcano, a hurricane, a manatee, or a Tyrannosaurus rex.

Think you might want to try it? Writing through a mask challenges you to use your imagination. You will need to introduce yourself and explain what you eat, where you live, and who your friends and enemies are. Teach us all about who you are. Good luck!

Writing an Acrostic Information Poem

RESOURCE MATERIAL

❧ Large chart

DISCUSSION

Okay, so we confess that we're not wild about acrostic poetry as poetry. The resulting poetry often sounds pretty awkward and stilted. But acrostic poems are a fun way for children to stretch the language they use. And an acrostic poem can provide a simple, contained way for students to organize the information they collect. It gives students just enough scaffolding for them to write about their topics.

HOW TO TEACH IT

We've been talking about different ways to write about what you've been learning about. Today we're going to talk about a new way. Does anyone here know what an acrostic poem is?

(Discuss.)

It's fun to use an acrostic poem in information writing, too. Let's say that you're studying sharks and want to try an acrostic poem. Begin by writing the word *shark* on your paper, like this.

(Demonstrate on a large piece of paper.)

Now you have to think about what you know about a shark, and how you could use these letters to write a poem that makes sense. Shall we try it together with *shark*?

(Work together with kids. When you're finished, the class poem might look something like this:)

Swimming through the ocean
Hungry and ferocious,
Always ready to strike,
Restlessly searching,
Keeping other fish on their toes!

Some of you might like to try this with the animal you've been learning about. Remember that the trick is to use each letter to start a line that will teach us about your animal.

Designing a Question/Answer Book

RESOURCE MATERIAL

❧ *Who Hoots?* by Katie Davis

DISCUSSION

Simple, predictable pattern books are used not only to teach children to read, but also by many nonfiction authors to entertain and teach young audiences. The question-and-answer format is an easy one for students to use. This craft lesson highlights a book that uses a playful variation on the simple question-and-answer format.

HOW TO TEACH IT

We've talked about patterns before and how they are found all around us. There may be a pattern in the tiles on a floor or a wall. In math we make patterns with numbers. Some books have patterns in them, too. Writers use patterns because they can be fun for readers to read. I'm going to read you Katie Davis's book *Who Hoots?* We've listened to this book before, but this time I want you to listen for the pattern.

(Read *Who Hoots?*)

In this book the author uses a question-and-answer pattern. She asks a question and then gives the answer. But she doesn't give us the answer right away. She tells us three things that don't hoot. Then she teases us by telling us a wrong answer when she says that owls don't hoot. Finally we turn the page and learn that owls *do* hoot, and then she adds one other fact about owls. The pattern repeats itself five times. By the end of the book we have learned who does and doesn't hoot, buzz, squeak, roar, and quack.

Katie Davis's pattern makes the book fun to read. Not all books have patterns, and not all pattern books have the one Katie Davis invented. If you want to use a pattern you get to create one that is special to your book. If you've written something and you like the way you wrote it, you might see if there's a way to repeat it to make a pattern. The question-and-answer pattern is a fun one to try.

Drawing on Personal Experience

RESOURCE MATERIAL

🐾 *The Pet Tarantula* by Marie Gibson

DISCUSSION

The research world of picture books, articles, *Weekly Reader,* multimedia encyclopedias on CD-ROM, nature films, and so on can be overwhelming to young writers. As we immerse them in the voices of other experts, we should take care that their own voices, perceptions, and observations don't get lost in the process. As students begin investigating their subjects, we need to make sure they value their own experience of the world.

HOW TO TEACH IT

You have been researching and learning about your topics from lots of experts. Today I want us to talk about the one expert who may be the most important of all.

You!

You have to be alive to what you're writing about. If you're writing about the stars, you'll learn a lot from books, but you shouldn't stop there. How else could you learn?

(Discuss.)

You could go outside at night, study the stars, and look through binoculars or a telescope if you have one. Maybe you remember that one summer night you saw lots of falling stars. What did that look like?

I have a book about tarantulas I'd like to share.

(Read *The Pet Tarantula* by Marie Gibson.)

You'll notice that the author adds things that she discovered while learning about tarantulas. You can do the same thing with what you're writing about. Let's say you're researching bees. Let's say you became interested because you are allergic to bees. Even if it doesn't talk about that in any of the books you've been reading, you can still add that to your writing.

When I read your writing, I don't want to hear only what the experts have to say. I want to find out what *you* think, what *you* noticed, what amazing things *you* know about your subject.

Using a Story to Teach Information

RESOURCE MATERIAL

☙ *Box Turtle at Long Pond* by William T. George

DISCUSSION

Many primary children have a pretty strong sense of story. We should help them get a sense of the difference between narrative and nonfiction, but at the same time we can build on their sense of story when we introduce them to information writing. There are many examples of information storybooks accessible for young readers. In these books the story often exists as a backdrop for teaching about the subject.

HOW TO TEACH IT

We have been talking about how teaching books are different from storybooks. But sometimes telling a story can be a great way of teaching about your topic.

Let's take a look at *Box Turtle at Long Pond* by William T. George. (Read the book.)

What did you learn about box turtles?

(Discuss. Make a list on a large chart.)

You may have noticed that the author teaches us about box turtles by telling us the story of what happened to one box turtle. The story takes place in one day. We learn about this box turtle through the words, but also through the pictures.

Do you think this might be a good way you could teach readers about your animal? When you tell a story you have to pick one or two of the animals, and get them doing something, such as looking for food, protecting themselves, taking care of their babies. While you're writing your story, see if you can teach us some facts about your animal, just like the author does in *Box Turtle at Long Pond*.

Beginning with the Setting

RESOURCE MATERIAL

🕮 None

DISCUSSION

Just as young children's drawings often show objects divorced from their setting, their nonfiction writing may lack a sense of place. Although not all nonfiction starts here, describing the setting is one way writers may choose to begin. Here's how you can introduce this concept to young writers.

HOW TO TEACH IT

As you've been gathering information about your topic, some of you may have been wondering what you should write about first. Sometimes writers begin by simply stating what they are writing about. For example, you might write, "This is a book about turtles." Although this beginning tells your readers what to expect, it might not get them excited about the topic.

One way to get readers interested is to bring them to the place where they can see the subject in its natural environment. I don't mean really bringing them; I mean using words to describe that place. For instance, if you were writing about turtles you might begin by describing the setting where a turtle might live:

> It is early morning and the birds are beginning to waken. They sip water from small pools from the leaf-covered ground. The air is still and quiet. Suddenly, a thrashing in the underbrush frightens a nearby squirrel. The squirrel scampers up the trunk of a tree while at the bottom, a brown head pokes itself out from beneath a rotting piece of bark. Turtle is awake.

When you begin by describing the setting, you invite the reader in for a closer look at your subject. To do this, you'll need first to think about the natural setting for your topic. If you are studying an animal, it will be the animal's habitat. If you are studying something like a planet, you'll have to try to take us to that planet by writing good description.

To get started, it may help to begin by writing a list of words that describe your setting. After warming up with your word list, see if you can write a description that will put your reader right in the setting of your subject.

Using Comparisons

RESOURCE MATERIAL

❧ *The Honey Makers* by Gail Gibbons

❧ *Sea Turtles* by Gail Gibbons

DISCUSSION

Nonfiction writing requires many skills, not the least of which is connecting, comparing, and contrasting factual information. It's hard to fathom the vastness of the universe or the size of a molecule. But when you compare such things to other, familiar objects, readers can use what they know to understand the unfamiliar.

HOW TO TEACH IT

You've been learning some very interesting facts about the topics you are studying. Sometimes these facts are hard to explain to a reader. For instance, if you write that a queen bee lays very small eggs, it doesn't help the reader know exactly how small. Or if you describe the size of a turtle, it isn't enough to say that the turtle is really, really big.

Writers often use comparisons to show exactly what they mean. When you compare one thing to another, it allows you to be very specific about the information. You'll find comparisons in many of the nonfiction books you read. Here are two examples, one about honeybees and one about turtles.

In *The Honey Makers* Gail Gibbons writes, "Most eggs the queen lays are no bigger than the period at the end of this sentence."

We all know how big a period is, so the comparison helps us know the size of the queen's eggs. In another book by Gail Gibbons, *Sea Turtles,* the author describes the prehistoric turtle, the Archelon, like this: "Archelon was so big that if it were still alive today a car could park between its flippers."

Because we know how big cars are, we can perfectly imagine the size of this turtle. When you try to describe something—whether how big or small it is or how shiny or blue—you can use a comparison to help your reader make a clearer picture of that thing. As you read your work, look for places where you can use comparisons to help you describe.

Repeating a Key Line

RESOURCE MATERIAL

❧ *An Egg Is an Egg* by Nicki Weiss

❧ *The Sun Is My Favorite Star* by Frank Asch

DISCUSSION

A writer can use a number of approaches to convey an important idea to readers. One simple tool is to select a line that represents a key idea and repeat it throughout the text. Young children can use this strategy to first identify, then reinforce a main idea.

HOW TO TEACH IT

How many of you know a song that has a part that repeats? In "Old MacDonald" we may sing a lot of different verses, but we always come back to the same line between each verse. "Old MacDonald had a farm, ee-ei-ee-ei-o." Lines that repeat are called refrains. Sometimes books will use refrains, too. A writer will repeat a line or two in the same way lines repeat in a song. Listen to this book, *An Egg Is an Egg,* by Nicki Weiss.

(Read and discuss.)

Did you notice the part that repeated? "Nothing stays the same. Everything can change." The author chose to repeat those lines because a lot of the book is about how things change. Nicki Weiss shows us how two things change, then writes her refrain. Then she shows us another two things that change and returns to her refrain. The refrain helps the reader pay attention to what the writer feels is most important. This book had a little surprise at the end, didn't it? Sometimes writers will change the refrain as a way to end the song or book.

(Note: *The Sun Is My Favorite Star* by Frank Asch is another book that models this craft lesson.)

If you have one idea that is most important to get across, you may want to use a repeating line or two like this author did. Read over your work. You may have already written a line that tells this most important idea. If you find a line or two, put a check mark next to it and think about where and when you could repeat it.

Speaking Directly to the Reader

RESOURCE MATERIAL

❧ *Bats! Strange and Wonderful* by Laurence Pringle

❧ *Are You a Snail?* by Judy Allen

DISCUSSION

You could define voice as an intimacy or closeness between writer and subject, writer and reader. Voice, or the lack thereof, isn't usually a huge problem with primary writers. But in their haste to write about their subject, young writers have a tendency to forget about the reader. This craft lesson shows how they can bring the reader into the writing.

HOW TO TEACH IT

When you're working on a piece of nonfiction writing, you need to concentrate on the subject you've been learning about. But you can't forget the reader, either. It's the reader who's going to hear what you have to say. Today we're going to talk about how you can speak directly to the reader in your writing.

Let's take another look at *Bats!* by Laurence Pringle. Here's the first page:

> If you were a bat, you could stay up all night. You could hang by your thumbs, or hang upside down by your toenails. You could fly through dark woods and even darker caves and not bump into anything.

(Note: *Are You a Snail?* by Judy Allen is another book that models this craft lesson.)

What did you notice about how the author wrote this page? (Discuss.)

Laurence Pringle speaks to us as readers. He makes it sound as though he were talking to us. Also, he asks us to imagine that we are bats, and what that might be like.

Do you think you might like to try writing by talking to the reader the way Laurence Pringle does? How might you do that? What would you say? Today I want you to think of a way you can include us readers and make us feel like we're part of your writing.

Supporting Details

K–2

RESOURCE
MATERIAL

❧ *Exploding Ants:*
Amazing Facts
About How
Animals Adapt by
Joanne Settel

DISCUSSION

Young writers often throw big ideas onto the paper and then forget to follow them up with supporting details. Learning to develop an idea is an important skill for the nonfiction writer.

HOW TO TEACH IT

I know some of you play soccer. When you get the soccer ball it's often tempting to kick it as hard as you can. But to get it farther down the field it's really better to give it a smaller kick and then to stay with it, kicking it a few more times before you pass it off to someone else on your team.

Writing is a little like soccer. Sometimes you have an exciting idea—a big idea—and you put it on the paper and then move on to something else. But just as with the soccer ball, it's better to stay with the big idea by adding a few more sentences to help explain it to the reader.

Listen to how this writer begins her book, *Exploding Ants: Amazing Facts About How Animals Adapt*:

Animals often do things that seem gross to us.

That's a pretty interesting idea. Doesn't it make you want to know more? Well, instead of just leaving us with the big idea, the writer follows up with a few details to help support the big idea. We call these "supporting details," and readers love them because they help them understand the interesting idea in more detail. Here's the big idea with three supporting details:

Animals often do things that seem gross to us. They eat foods that people would find nauseating. They make their homes in disgusting places and feed on mucus and blood. They swell or blow up their body parts.

Notice the difference? When you go back to read your writing today, I want you to look and see if you wrote some big ideas that need following up. If you find any, underline them. When I confer with you today I'll help you think about how to follow up those sentences with supporting details.

Writing with Voice

RESOURCE MATERIAL

❧ "All about thee oyl sPil" by Lauren Loewy (Appendix C)

DISCUSSION

We're defining voice in writing as "personality-on-paper." Voiceless writing is less of a problem in the primary grades than it is in the upper grades. But when primary children move from personal narratives and attempt to write about factual information, you may notice that the voice in their writing starts to disappear. They put their feelings and reactions on hold and fall back on listing or repeating rather than really explaining. One of the best antidotes for this problem is to show models from other children's information writing. It's important to make time to talk about these examples and what can be learned from them.

HOW TO TEACH IT

Whenever you write, you want your readers to feel as though you were speaking to them. That's true when you write a story, but it's also true when you write a teaching book.

Today I want to share a story that was written by a first grader named Lauren Loewy. About ten years ago a big oil tanker named the Exxon Valdez had an accident in Alaska and spilled many gallons of oil. Some of you may know about this. The oil clogged up the beaches. The sad thing is that many birds and other ocean animals died. Let's listen to Lauren's teaching book.

(Read "All about thee oyl sPil" in Appendix C.)

Let's talk about Lauren's story. What did she teach us about what happened?

(Discuss.)

What else did she tell us? How did she feel about this accident?

(Discuss.)

Today I want you to think about Lauren's story as you work on your own teaching books. You want to teach certain facts to your reader, but at the same time you want to let your own writing voice come through the words.

Nonfiction Craft Lessons 3–4

*T*he third-grade students clustered around their teacher. She was reading them *Bugs,* Parker and Wright's information picture book that covers a parade of insects familiar to children. They were having fun guessing the answers to the riddles: What crawled into Grant's shirt and pants? (Ants.) What did Sam find swimming in his apple cider? (A spider.)

Suddenly Jacob started talking, spilling everything he knew about spiders. And he knew a lot. He knew that there are about 30,000 different kinds of spiders in the world and that most of them aren't harmful. He knew that they "peeled out of their skin when their bodies grew bigger." And he told us some spiders jump far and spit poison on the bugs they catch. When he finished, his teacher looked at him and said, "I bet you could write a teaching book about spiders yourself!" Jacob beamed and settled back comfortably to finish listening to the rest of the story.

Third- and fourth-grade students bring particular strengths to the world of nonfiction writing. Like younger children, they continue to show interest in the world around them. But unlike their younger brothers and sisters, they are often armed with more than what they have learned from experience. Jacob didn't gather everything he knew about spiders from firsthand experience. He had learned it watching television, looking at pictures in books and magazines, and reading about them himself. This era of content confidence makes nonfiction writing a natural for many students this age.

Students often hit their stride as fluent readers sometime during the years of third and fourth grade. Now they can grapple with more difficult texts, making it easier to delve into the print world to research their interests. As readers, they have discovered nonfiction as well. Led by their curiosity about the world, and bolstered by stronger reading ability, many kids this age choose to read nonfiction exclusively. Inviting students to write in this genre allows us to tap the resource of their reading. When we ask students, "How has this writer helped you learn about this subject?" we invite them to bring a reader's perspective to the writer's task. Because many are immersed in these books, the time is ripe to lead them into a study of nonfiction writing.

Students of this age bring other resources to the table. In the introduction to the K–2 section we wrote about the mismatch between Joseph's desire to research monkeys and his ability to do so. Although this mismatch may still exist for the third and fourth grader, the extra years have helped close the gap. Kids this age are natural collectors. They know how to sort and categorize their trading cards. They can distinguish between the rare and ordinary shells in a collection from the beach. They can gather and summarize, understand cause and effect, and begin to weave together relationships among distinct facts.

Whereas younger children often blend the world of the subject with their own worlds—without seeing the edges of either—third and fourth graders are more able to recognize that research involves looking beyond the world as they know it. They are eager to dive into a pile of books to gather new facts. At the same time, students may fail to value the knowledge they bring to the subject. We can help with this. The lesson about uncovering prior knowledge shows one way how.

In his book *Writing to Learn,* William Zinsser talks about two kinds of writing: Type A (expert) and Type B (exploratory). He argues that the quality of expert writing depends on a great deal of exploratory writing. We agree! Most third- and fourth-grade writers are able to grasp the concept of exploratory writing. They understand the difference between exploratory writing in a research journal (freewriting, question generating, note taking, reacting to notes, flash drafts) and writing for the final presentation. Encourage your students to use exploratory writing to "juice" the information they are taking in. This leads to clearer thinking and helps students bring more voice and insight to their final product.

Finally a word about the workshop time. We believe in giving students a regular, predictable time to write about topics of their choice. Having said that, we notice that students sometimes bypass using this time to explore their interests and passions. When it's time to write, students may forget about their burgeoning interest in rocks and minerals that was ignited in science earlier in the day. They may forget the fury they felt outside at recess when the jump rope competition they organized fell apart because the rules weren't written down. Students can easily compartmentalize their learning along the same lines of a fragmented school day. We can remind them that the workshop gives them time to pursue the interests and purposes they have as they live in the big, wide world of school and home.

Exploratory: Using Questions to Outline

RESOURCE MATERIAL

❧ *Write to Learn* by Donald Murray

❧ Questions you generate about a topic of interest to you

DISCUSSION

Can any of us forget the dreaded formal outline teachers asked us to complete before writing? In his book *Write to Learn,* Donald Murray suggests eleven alternatives to the formal outline and offers this piece of advice: "None of these is *the* way to outline. Develop your own system of outlining. Outline only if it helps you, and then outline in a way that provides that help" (p. 100).

In the next two lessons we offer two of Murray's strategies that are simple enough for young writers to use.

HOW TO TEACH IT

A simple way to organize your writing is to consider the questions a reader will have about your subject. I've been thinking about writing a book about saltwater taffy. Ever since I was little I've been going to this shop in the summer where I can watch the taffy makers work. I've been researching this topic a bit. Today I'm going to think about the questions my readers might ask:

> Why do they call it saltwater taffy? Is there really salt in it?
> How do they make it?
> What flavors can you get?
> When did they first start making this kind of candy?
> Why do people love it?
> Why does it come in different shapes?
> What is saltwater taffy?

The next thing I'll do is put these questions in order by thinking about what the reader might need or want to know first and so on. (Place numbers next to the questions as you talk about each.)

I think it makes sense to begin with the last question, What is saltwater taffy? Then I'll move to the question, When did they first start making this kind of candy? From there I'll write about how they make it, what flavors they have, and why it comes in different shapes. And for the last question, I'll give my opinion on why so many people love it.

Now I have a road map that will guide me as I start to write. I may find the need to change as I go along and that's okay. But for now, this helps me get started.

If you are thinking about how to organize your writing, you might give this strategy a try. See if it works for you!

Exploratory: Outlining the Beginning, Middle, and End

RESOURCE MATERIAL

☙ Appendixes D1 and D2

DISCUSSION

Children are accustomed to thinking in terms of beginning, middle, and end when writing stories. They can use the same thought in organizing their nonfiction writing. Here's another prewriting strategy Don Murray borrows from his friend Donald Graves.

HOW TO TEACH IT

(Copy the chart in Appendix D1 onto a large sheet of paper.)

Today I want to share one way to organize information before writing. Take a look at the chart I have. Let's say I'm planning to write about tsunamis. In the first column, Brainstorming, I'll list all the information I want to include. Let's take a look at it together.

Next, I'll read each idea and think about whether it should go in the beginning, the middle, or the end of my paper.

(Demonstrate this in front of students, using arrows to show where each bit of information belongs. Appendix D2 shows a completed example of this chart for the topic of tsunamis.)

There are copies of this chart at the writing area. If you are ready to begin writing, you might try using this strategy to help order your information.

Jazzing Up Your Title

RESOURCE MATERIAL

❧ *It's Disgusting and We Ate It! True Food Facts from Around the World and Throughout History* by James Solheim

DISCUSSION

As students learn about their particular topics, they will revise their thinking many times along the way. Revising the title is one of the simplest examples of this. On one hand, changing a title is easy since the title is so short. We want to teach kids that a snappy title will entice their readers. But the title is more than window dressing. We have often seen that when students sharpen their titles, it has a positive effect on the entire piece of writing.

HOW TO TEACH IT

Today I want you to think about your title. Often we don't really think much about it. We come up with a title that is nothing more than a label, like a tag that gets stuck on a holiday present. A title like "Bees" or "Slavery" is okay for a start, but at some point you probably want to come up with a title that's going to intrigue your readers.

Consider these ideas for jazzing up your title. (You might want to list these on a large easel.)

1. Surprise your reader: "Rabbits That Kill," "They Bloom Only at Night."

2. Use humor: *It's Disgusting and We Ate It!* or "Don't Marry a Black Widow Spider."

3. Try using an adjective that starts with the same letter as your subject: "The Terrifying Tarantula" or "Mischievous Monkeys." This technique is called *alliteration* in poetry, and it can create a title that is fun to say out loud.

Take a good hard look at your title. Is it just a label, or will it really grab your readers' attention and make them want to read more? If you want to jazz up your title, consider using one of these ideas.

Remember: your title should be as specific as possible. If your title is too general ("Dinosaurs" or "Pollution"), it's probably a sign that you need to focus your topic by taking a slice instead of the whole thing. Instead of "Predators," for example, you might want to narrow your title to "Predators of the Night."

Writing Subtitles That Teach

RESOURCE MATERIAL

❧ *It's Disgusting and We Ate It! True Food Facts from Around the World and Throughout History* by James Solheim

❧ *Exploding Ants: Amazing Facts About How Animals Adapt* by Joanne Settel

❧ *Gold: The True Story of Why People Search for It, Mine It, Trade It, Steal It, Mint It, Hoard It, Shape It, Wear It, Fight and Kill for It* by Milton Meltzer

DISCUSSION

Writers are resourceful people. They recognize that each element, including the title of a text, has an important job to do. In this craft lesson we show how a subtitle can be used to explain the particular angle the student will take on the topic.

HOW TO TEACH IT

A title will help the reader enter the world the writer is exploring. A good title grabs a reader's attention and tells him what to expect. That's a lot to accomplish for something as small as a title. One way writers do this is by writing a *subtitle*. A subtitle follows the main title and is used to give the reader additional information. In these examples you can see that each writer uses the main title to get the reader interested. The subtitle follows with a more detailed explanation of what the book promises to deliver.

> *It's Disgusting and We Ate It!: True Food Facts from Around the World and Throughout History*
> *Exploding Ants: Amazing Facts About How Animals Adapt*
> *Gold: The True Story of Why People Search for It, Mine It, Trade It, Steal It, Mint It, Hoard It, Shape It, Wear It, Fight and Kill for It*

As you can see, writers aren't afraid to write long subtitles!

Take a look at your title. Have you chosen one that will grab the reader's attention and signal what is coming next? If not, would it help to use a subtitle?

Narrowing Your Focus

RESOURCE MATERIAL

☙ *Poison Dart Frogs* by Jennifer Owings Dewey

DISCUSSION

We believe that teachers should give students as much choice as possible in nonfiction writing. But many kids get bogged down by general topics about which you could write not just one book, but a whole series! This is not surprising when we assign each student to write about a general topic—a particular state, for example. Such topics often lead to flat, laundry-list writing. It's our job to help students find topics that are manageable in size and scope.

HOW TO TEACH IT

I want to tell you a little story about a fourth-grade boy named Owen. The kids in Owen's class were going to write an information report on a subject that interested them. His teacher took the class to the library and let the students decide what they wanted to write about. Owen did a little research and made his decision: "I'm going to write about the universe."

He dragged a ton of books back to the classroom and started to research.

"How's it going?" his teacher asked after two days.

"It's too much!" he moaned. "I think I'm just going to concentrate on our solar system."

Owen kept narrowing and narrowing his topic. Finally he ended up writing about Ganymede, which is Jupiter's largest moon. He did a fine piece of writing.

When you write nonfiction you need to focus your topic until you find a particular angle that seems right. Take a slice of the pie. The universe was too big a topic for Owen to research, but he became an expert on one of Jupiter's moons.

Jennifer Owings Dewey writes information books. She could have written a book about amphibians, but instead she decided to write about frogs. In fact, she wrote about one kind of frog—poison dart frogs.

Today I want you to think about your topic. Is it too broad and general? Would it make sense to try to narrow your focus? That's something that we might talk about today as I come around to confer with you.

Focusing on the One

RESOURCE MATERIAL

🐾 *A Caribou Journey* by Debbie S. Miller

🐾 *Arlene Sardine* by Christopher Raschka

DISCUSSION

As kids get older curricular demands increase. School gets harder and harder. Young information writers are asked to grapple with alien concepts and topics well outside their own experiences. No wonder they tend to produce writing that feels cold and detached. We need to give students strategies for personalizing their material. Here's one of the best ways we know.

HOW TO TEACH IT

As you research, you have dug up lots of facts about your subjects. It can be tempting to bury your reader in facts—thousands of comets, millions of starfish, billions of lobster eggs . . . These facts may be very important, but don't forget that it's hard for readers to wrap their minds around these mind-boggling numbers.

Today I'm going to suggest one way you can deal with this problem. Instead of writing about your subject in general, select *one* animal, person, or thing to write about. To do that, you need to create a few scenes in which you can describe it. You can teach all about your topic by focusing on the one, and using it as an example.

Let's take another look at the book *A Caribou Journey*. The author could have simply provided a list of facts about caribou. Instead, she begins by describing one caribou mother with her son:

> On a windswept ridge, a small group of caribou plods through the crusted snow. One caribou mother digs a small crater with her broad, sharp-edged hooves. She smells lichens beneath the snow. Her calf paws through the snow next to her. The young bull has learned to dig for his food by watching his mother.

We learn all about the life cycle of the caribou by watching this mother and her son. Chris Raschka does the same thing in his book *Arlene Sardine*. You remember that this book teaches us about how sardines end up in a can. Raschka creates a single character, Arlene, and lets us get to know and care about her. This makes the book come alive.

I want you to reread your material and ask yourself if it might be a good idea to focus on one of what you're writing about. If you do that, you'll want to create a real character with feelings, needs, frustrations, and attitude. Go to it!

Writing an Introduction

RESOURCE MATERIAL

❧ *All About Rattlesnakes* by Jim Arnosky

❧ *Brain Surgery for Beginners and Other Major Operations for Minors* by Steve Parker

❧ "Guide for a Clean Outhouse" by Marnie Wells (Appendix E)

DISCUSSION

The introduction is a chance for young writers to state in a simple, concise form what the piece will be about. After you teach this idea, keep a wary eye out for formulaic writing in which all your students' introductions begin to sound the same. If that starts to happen, you may want to show them examples of different kinds of introductions. It's important that they get a sense of the range of options available for writing an introduction.

HOW TO TEACH IT

(Start by reading the one-page introduction from *Brain Surgery for Beginners and Other Major Operations for Minors.*)

Are you interested? I read that because today we're going to talk about writing an introduction. When I say *introduction* I mean the opening sentences, or paragraphs, of a piece of writing. Think of it as shaking hands with a new person, your reader, for the first time. It's an important first connection.

You can write different kinds of introductions. The one I just read had a humorous, playful tone. Here's another book, *All About Rattlesnakes* by Jim Arnosky. His introduction begins with five questions and his promise to answer them in the book.

Marnie Wells, an eighth grader, wrote a how-to guide for an unlikely subject—how to clean an outhouse! Here's how she begins:

> This pamphlet is your guide to quick and easy outhouse cleaning.
> Your sparkling, fresh-smelling outhouse can be the envy of all your neighbors.
> Guests will remark that your privy is the best that they have ever visited.
> If you want to hear all sorts of wonderful things about your outhouse, read the following pages carefully and enjoy with the author's compliments . . .

Think about the introduction you'll want to write for your own information piece. The introduction you write should do these things:

- Explain your purpose for writing it.
- State the main ideas that will follow.
- Get your reader interested.

Think about the kind of introduction you'll want to write for your information piece.

Writing in Paragraph Form

RESOURCE MATERIAL

☙ Appendixes F1 and F2

DISCUSSION

Although the reminder to indent often comes as students write their final drafts, thinking in paragraphs also helps the writer to organize information. Paragraphs are an organizational tool. They make writing "easy on the reader's eye" and help writers be clear about what they think and feel. It takes years of experience to develop the skill of using paragraphs well. Here's a way to introduce students to the purpose and process of using them in their writing.

HOW TO TEACH IT

(Place Appendixes F1 and F2 on an overhead projector or make copies so students can see the examples you will be referring to.)

Let's take a look at these two pages. They say exactly the same thing, but before you read either one I want you to think about something. If you came across these two pages and were going to read only one of them, which one do you think you'd pick?

Most of us would read this one (Appendix F2) because it looks easier to read. Reading this one (Appendix F1) feels a little like swimming underwater while holding your breath. There's no place to stop and come up for air. Paragraphs give readers a break. They also help organize information. Each paragraph usually has its own topic or central idea. Let's read the passage and see what that looks like.

I'll read this page aloud twice. The first time just listen and enjoy. The second time through I'll stop after each paragraph and consider what topic or idea is central to each paragraph.

(Help students visualize this by circling each paragraph after you read. Next to it write a key word or phrase that summarizes each central idea.)

Paragraphs make the page "friendlier" to the reader's eye and easier to understand because the information is organized around separate ideas. When you are writing today, try organizing your information into paragraphs. Begin writing about one thing (for example, the kinds of food your animal likes to eat), then indent and begin a new paragraph when you switch to a new idea (such as the different places it uses for shelter).

Writing a Topic Sentence

RESOURCE MATERIAL

❧ "Saltwater Taffy" (Appendix G) or writing you generate as an example

DISCUSSION

You've introduced the concept of paragraphs and invited students to use them when writing. Some are bound to use them incorrectly. One reason is that students sometimes have underdeveloped ideas. They write one sentence and are ready to move on to another topic. Although not all paragraphs require topic sentences, many expository texts do use topic sentences as organizers. Learning to recognize and use a topic sentence can help students develop their ideas.

HOW TO TEACH IT

Earlier we talked about paragraphs, and I've noticed many of you using them to help organize your writing. I've noticed that some of you have trouble deciding when one paragraph should end and another should begin. Using a topic sentence can make this decision easier. A topic sentence is one sentence that clearly states the main idea of the paragraph. Here's an example:

(Share text from Appendix G or generate something on your own.)

Saltwater taffy has been around a long time is the topic sentence in this paragraph. It tells you what the rest of the paragraph will be about. As we read on we learn about how far back it goes and where it may have come from.

If you wanted to talk about the different flavors of taffy it wouldn't make sense to put it in this paragraph. Let's write a new topic sentence for a paragraph that will describe the different flavors.

Saltwater taffy comes in lots of different flavors. There are the flavors that most of us think about when we think of taffy: molasses, peppermint, vanilla, chocolate, and strawberry. But what about raspberry lemonade, piña colada, and banana creme pie? The number of saltwater taffy flavors is growing because there are new and easier ways to add flavor to recipes.

If you aren't sure when to start a new paragraph, it may be because you aren't organizing your writing around a series of main ideas. Writing a topic sentence helps you focus on one main idea at a time. Try stating your main idea in a topic sentence and then continue the paragraph by explaining more about that sentence. When you are ready to shift to another main idea, write a new topic sentence.

Copyright © 2001

JoAnn Portalupi and

Ralph Fletcher.

Stenhouse Publishers

Using Subheadings to Organize Information

RESOURCE MATERIAL

≈ *The Top of the World: Climbing Mt. Everest* by Steve Jenkins

DISCUSSION

Whenever we look at nonfiction books we find ourselves getting excited about those with text features that seem particularly accessible to students. The book cited here, *The Top of the World: Climbing Mt. Everest* by Steve Jenkins, has much to teach our nonfiction writers. But this craft lesson focuses on the subheading as a way to help students present their information in a clear and organized manner.

HOW TO TEACH IT

Today we're going to study a nonfiction picture book—*The Top of the World: Climbing Mt. Everest* by Steve Jenkins.

(Read book.)

What did you notice about the way the author wrote this book? (Discuss.)

You were struck by the unusual illustrations made from paper cutouts. But you also may have noticed that at the top of each page you find what looks like a chapter title, in bold print. This is called a subheading. Steve Jenkins uses it to organize his material. On one page the subheading is "Packing for the Trip" and underneath you see all the equipment you'll need. On another page the subheading is "Avalanche," and you learn that most people who die on Mt. Everest are victims of avalanches.

Subheadings help you structure or "chunk" your material. They help keep you organized when you write. Readers appreciate them, too, because they know where to find what they're looking for. Can you think of other books that use subheadings?

(Discuss.)

Think about whether you want to use subheadings in your nonfiction writing. What would the subheadings be?

Describing Your Subject

RESOURCE MATERIAL

⊱ *Lincoln: A Photobiography* by Russell Freedman

⊱ *Dakota Dugout* by Ann Turner

DISCUSSION

We think of description as a skill needed for writing stories or poems. But it's at least as important to nonfiction writing. Young writers need to help their readers picture what they're writing about. Drawings and photographs will help, but these visual aids can't replace the need for a written description.

Teachers need to remind students to take the time to describe the person, animal, place, or historical event that they are writing about. This will improve the quality of their writing. And it should be mentioned that writing tests in many states ask students to write a "descriptive paragraph" about a topic.

HOW TO TEACH IT

You've been doing lots of research. Sometimes when you have spent lots of time researching, you get to the point that you can picture exactly what you're writing about. It's easy to forget that your readers, who haven't done the same research, need your help to get a "mind picture" of your topic.

Let's take a look at two writers who take the time to describe their subjects. *Lincoln: A Photobiography* by Russell Freedman contains many wonderful drawings and photographs. But the author knows he can't rely only on these pictures. He describes his subject. In fact the book begins like this:

> Abraham Lincoln wasn't the sort of man who could lose himself in a crowd. After all, he stood six feet four inches tall, and to top it off, he wore a high silk hat.
>
> His height was mostly in his long bony legs. When he sat in a chair, he seemed no taller than anyone else. It was only when he stood up that he towered above other men.

(As another example, look at the descriptions in Ann Turner's *Dakota Dugout*.)

Here's my challenge: reread your writing and see if you have described your subject. If not, I want you to use your words to paint a picture of what you're writing about. Remember: the five senses are important tools when it comes to creating a "mind picture" for the reader. When I confer with you, I'll be interested in hearing where in your piece you're going to put this description.

Using Supporting Details and Examples

RESOURCE MATERIAL

🐾 *Animal Dads*
by Sneed B.
Collard III

DISCUSSION

Students too often make unsupported claims in their nonfiction writing: *The computer saves us time.* (How?) *Hockey is the most challenging sport.* (In what respect?) We need to impress upon students that in the "food chain of ideas," big ideas are nourished by specifics: smaller details and concrete examples. By providing supporting details, students ground their writing in the real world. This gives it authority. It is also a good way to help students flesh out skimpy or underdeveloped writing.

HOW TO TEACH IT

When you write nonfiction, beware that you don't make statements without backing them up with evidence. Let's say that your subject is World War II and you write

> World War II was the most destructive war in the history of the planet. Today, we must do whatever we can to make sure that nothing like that ever happens again.

That's a noble idea, but the author didn't give us a single fact or bit of evidence to support the statement that World War II was the most destructive war in history. What about the First World War? What about Vietnam? Those kinds of unsupported statements weaken a piece of nonfiction writing.

Today let's take a look at *Animal Dads*. This book does many things well, but today as I reread it to you, I'd like you to pay attention to how the author backs up his statements with examples and concrete details. (Read. Discuss.)

Today I want you to consider this idea as you revisit your writing. Have you done what Sneed B. Collard does? If you are just beginning to write, remember to back up your ideas with enough examples, details, and facts.

Leaving Out What the Reader Already Knows

RESOURCE MATERIAL

🐾 "Rabbits"
(Appendix H)

DISCUSSION

Redundancy must be considered a prime suspect for the limpness in most students' nonfiction writing. The writer tells the readers not only what he or she has already said, but also what the readers already knew before they began reading. How to deal with this problem? First, make students aware of the reader, and give them practice at removing unnecessary parts. Pruning a piece of cluttered writing will breathe energy into it.

HOW TO TEACH IT

Nonfiction writing draws on a connection between three things. You need a writer—that's you. You need a topic—that's what you're learning and writing about. And you need readers. There's an unwritten contract between the writer and reader in which the reader says, *I'll keep reading your writing so long as you teach me about your subject and keep me interested. But don't take me for granted or you'll lose me. And then I'll go do something else.*

One sure way to bore your readers is to tell them what they already know. Let's take a look at this short piece about rabbits.

(See "Rabbits" in Appendix H.)

You should each have a copy of this. I'm going to read it out loud.

(Read.)

Now I want you to get into pairs. I want you to read the piece again, and I want you to put brackets around information that made you say to yourself, "Yeah, yeah, I already knew that!"

(Kids work together.)

What parts did you bracket? Do you see how much stronger this piece would have been if the author had left out those parts we already knew?

Think about this as you return to your writing. Read it over. Have you included parts that readers already know? If so, you may be able to cut it. Trust your reader! Remember: removing those parts shouldn't make your report shorter. Instead, it gives you a chance to go deeper, to tell us more about the interesting parts.

Using Commas to List Multiple Facts

RESOURCE MATERIAL

❦ "Commas in a List" (Appendix I)

❦ *Bats! Strange and Wonderful* by Laurence Pringle

DISCUSSION

Because a nonfiction text involves combining details and drawing relationships between various facts, it offers young writers the opportunity to stretch their abilities to write more complex sentences. Showing students how to use commas to list facts gives them a way to avoid simple, repetitive sentences.

HOW TO TEACH IT

Does anyone know what the word *efficient* means? If something is efficient it means that it does the job quickly and well. For instance, we've been working on learning how to move quickly and quietly from our desks to the carpet area. I could say we have found an efficient way to do that job.

I want to talk today about efficient sentences. An efficient sentence is a sentence that conveys information quickly and well. Consider the following facts about bats:

(These sentences and the one to follow should be printed on a chart.)

Bats live in tropical rain forests. They can also live in mountains. Bats live in deserts, too. They probably live right in your neighborhood.

I've used four sentences to teach that information. But because all the sentences teach about where bats live, there's a more efficient way to combine the information. Laurence Pringle wrote a sentence that combines all these facts.

Bats live in tropical rain forests, in mountains, in deserts, and probably right in your neighborhood.

What differences do you notice? (You could point out the fact that he uses only one sentence instead of four and that the commas allow him to list the information. We find it better to invite students to share their own discoveries. This doesn't mean you let go of what you plan to teach. If students do not discover Pringle's use of commas to list facts, share that observation with them as described below.)

Notice how this author uses commas to list the four places where bats may be. When you have more than two facts that group together around one idea, you can combine them by using commas like this author does. Notice that you put a comma after each fact. Just before you get to the last fact, you also use the word *and* to let the reader know the list is complete. Let's try it a couple of times to see how easy it is. (Appendix I offers three other clusters of simple, repetitive sentences that you can rewrite into single sentences using commas in a list.)

Putting Voice into Nonfiction Writing

RESOURCE MATERIAL

࿊ *Wolves* by Seymour Simon

࿊ Encyclopedia entry about wolves

DISCUSSION

The writing process movement has succeeded in energizing expressive writing (personal narrative, fiction, and poetry). But it seems to us that the writing pertaining to factual matters (reports, essays, content-area writing) has been left behind. This kind of writing tends to be dry, boring, and mechanical. Our challenge as teachers is to show students how they can breathe voice into their nonfiction writing. This craft lesson was suggested by Bev Gallagher.

HOW TO TEACH IT

Bev Gallagher teaches third grade at the Princeton Day School in New Jersey. She says, "One lesson that I love to teach is showing the kids options in nonfiction writing and picking out mentors. I photocopied the first couple of pages from *Wolves* by Seymour Simon. I did the same thing with the encyclopedia text entry on the same topic. The students and I talked about what we noticed. It was incredibly powerful for third graders to see the difference, and it led to an amazing conversation about voice."

Copyright © 2001

JoAnn Portalupi and

Ralph Fletcher.

Stenhouse Publishers

Putting the Reader into Your Writing

RESOURCE MATERIAL

🐌 *Are You a Snail?*
by Judy Allen

DISCUSSION

When we read a novel, we are asked to make a leap of the imagination to connect with the setting, the characters, and their struggles. But nonfiction readers must make a similar leap to enter the world of information being written about. Here's a technique young writers can use to help their readers make this leap of the imagination.

HOW TO TEACH IT

After doing your research, you start feeling like an expert, or at least an insider, on your subject. But remember: your reader is probably an outsider. Your reader hasn't spent nearly as much time as you have spent investigating this subject. Your challenge as you write is to figure out some way to include the reader, to bring him or her into what you're writing about.

One way you can do that is to ask your reader to imagine that he or she is the thing you are writing about. If you are writing about a famous person, ask the reader to imagine being that person at a particular time in history. If you are writing about an animal, ask the reader to imagine being that animal.

Here's one book that does a great job of doing just that.

(Read *Are You a Snail?* by Judy Allen.)

What did you notice about how the book was written?

(Discuss.)

You'll notice that this book was written in the second-person point of view: the "you." The author speaks directly to the reader. This is a very intimate way of writing.

As you work on your information report, I want you to consider trying this yourself. To do this well you're going to have to imagine what it would feel like to be the person or animal you are writing about. Use your imagination. It's a great way of putting voice into your writing.

Using Repetition for Emphasis

RESOURCE MATERIAL

❧ *Fish Faces* by Norbert Wu

DISCUSSION

When we read and write poetry with our students, we naturally attend to such qualities as rhythm, cadence, and word choice. We know that the sound of language is a tool poets use to produce poems that are pleasing to hear. But these qualities are not the realm of poets only. Simple strategies, such as repetition, can be used to enhance the aesthetics of nonfiction writing, too.

HOW TO TEACH IT

We've talked about how writers think not only about *what* to say, but also *how* to say it. They listen to the sounds of the language because how words sound influences whether readers find it interesting and pleasing. One strategy writers use to make their writing sound beautiful is repetition. This can make your writing sound more poetic. Also, repeating a certain word helps the reader hold on to the idea you want to get across.

We've read the book *Fish Faces* by Norbert Wu. Let's look at it again and pay attention to how he uses repetition to make the writing sing and to help the reader pay attention to what's important.

(On chart paper print the two passages below that describe mouths and noses of fish.)

> Fish with mouths that open wide
> Mouth like a tube, mouth like a beak
> Mouth that belongs to a monster of the deep
>
> A long nose, a flat nose, a hard-to-ignore nose
> A nose that looks like it could cut wood
> A nose that shines in the dark!

In each example the author has chosen one important word to repeat. Let's find each word and underline them. Why do you think he chose the words he did? In each case he chooses the word that names what he is focusing on in his description. Listen while I read each passage aloud, and pay attention to how the repetition makes the description sound.

Is there a place in your writing where you might use repetition to make it sound poetic? Is there a place where repetition could put the reader's focus right where you want it?

Using Comparisons

RESOURCE MATERIAL

❧ *The Moon and You* by E. C. Krupp

DISCUSSION

Nonfiction writing requires students to teach the information they have gathered on a subject. But many complicated concepts in the scientific or historical world are flat-out difficult to explain. In this craft lesson, we talk about comparing one thing to another. Here we encourage kids to look to the familiar when trying to explain alien ideas in their nonfiction writing.

HOW TO TEACH IT

When you write a "teaching book," you often have the challenge of trying to explain ideas that are complicated. The size of a blue whale, the speed of light, the total power output of a hurricane—it's hard for readers to understand such gigantic ideas!

If you're having trouble explaining these ideas, try comparing them to everyday ideas that will be familiar to the reader. Let's say, for example, you're writing about whales, and you want to describe the baleen plates whales use to eat krill or plankton. You might describe them as "vertical venetian blinds attached to the upper jaw." You are giving readers a familiar reference point to help them picture what you're talking about.

There's a good example of this in *The Moon and You* by E. C. Krupp. Throughout this book, the author makes comparisons between the moon and everyday life. For example, on the sixth page he writes:

> In a baseball game on the moon, every hit would be a home run. You would reach first base in about ten steps. The game would never be called on account of rain. With no air to carry the sound, you could never hear the fans cheer at Moon Stadium.

Later, to explain the relative size difference between the moon and the earth, he writes,

> If the moon were a tennis ball, the earth would be a basketball!

Try this idea. Reread your writing from the perspective of someone who knows little about your topic. If a certain idea seems unclear, try comparing it to something familiar.

Selecting Fascinating Facts

RESOURCE MATERIAL

❧ *All About Rattlesnakes* by Jim Arnosky

❧ *A Drop of Water: A Book of Science and Wonder* by Walter Wick

DISCUSSION

Crafting nonfiction writing involves learning how to sift the good stuff from the mundane. That's a big challenge for young writers who quickly get overwhelmed by too much information and go on automatic pilot as they struggle to copy it all down. In this craft lesson we talk about finding and using amazing facts or details. This skill is useful both while students are collecting information and when they are crafting the finished piece.

HOW TO TEACH IT

As you research, you will come across tons of information. Some facts will be things everybody already knows. Other facts will be boring. But you'll learn some things that will make you say, "Whoa! Can that really be true?" Pay attention when that happens, because fascinating facts make a piece of nonfiction writing come alive.

Let's take a look at a few books that use amazing facts. You'll remember *A Drop of Water* by Walter Wick. This book looks at water in many different forms. On page 15 he writes about bubbles:

> Its shimmering liquid is five hundred times thinner than a human hair.

Imagine! During his research Walter Wick must have dug up that astonishing fact. Later, he made sure to include it in his book.

Jim Arnosky includes some fascinating facts in *All About Rattlesnakes,* including this one:

> The rattlesnake's heat-sensing capability can detect and pinpoint prey, even in total darkness, as long as the prey animal's body temperature is warmer than its surroundings.

As a nonfiction writer, you'll want to be on the lookout for remarkable facts or details so you can include them in your final book or report. Pay attention to your own reaction. Chances are good that if you're amazed by a particular fact or detail, your readers will be amazed, too.

Writing a Strong Lead for a Biography

RESOURCE MATERIAL

❧ *Indian Chiefs* by Russell Freedman

❧ Transparency showing leads of different chapters in Freedman's book

DISCUSSION

In many third- and fourth-grade classrooms, students write biographies of important historic men and women. Such writing often comes out dry and flat, particularly the lead. As teachers, we need to do whatever we can to revitalize these leads. We have noticed that energizing the lead in a student's writing can have a nice echoing effect that carries to the very end.

HOW TO TEACH IT

Aimee Buckner teaches fourth grade at Brookwood Elementary School in Georgia. In this craft lesson, Aimee tries to attune her students to various ways of beginning their biographical writing:

> In order to help students to see that grabber leads count in biography reports, too, we study the beginnings of each chapter in Russell Freedman's book *Indian Chiefs*. I usually type all the leads onto one page and make a transparency for me and copies for the kids to use as a resource. We then read these first sentences and study how Freedman makes us want to read more about these Native Americans. He uses a variety of techniques, which we try to name. Freedman sometimes starts off with a childhood story, a quote from someone who knew the chief, a physical description of the chief, and even an active lead that puts the reader right in the middle of a battle. After we have looked at these leads and tried to name what Russell Freedman was trying to do, my students go back to the biography they are writing and rework their own beginnings.

Attending to Setting

RESOURCE
MATERIALS

❧ *Into the Sea* by
Brenda Z.
Guiberson

DISCUSSION

A young child's drawing often includes only the main object or event of the topic at hand. If a child writes about falling off a swing, you may see a sad-faced skeletal figure placed next to a swing. What if the story is about Mom? There she is, smiling and holding an oversized cooking spoon. Missing are the surrounding drawings that place the subject into a larger context, giving the reader a fuller, richer experience with the topic.

The same thing can be true when older writers work on their nonfiction. When they are so focused on their subjects, they often neglect the role setting can play in illuminating the subject for the reader.

HOW TO TEACH IT

We've talked about setting as one important part of a story. But the setting can play an important part in nonfiction writing as well. No matter what you are writing about, it has a certain place or way it fits into our world. You can think of this place as setting. For instance, if your topic is hamsters, ask yourself, Where do hamsters fit into the world? They are usually found as pets, at home, or in a classroom. If you are studying diamonds, the setting where they are found is deep underground. What about honeybees? They could be found in a meadow or maybe in your family's garden. Placing your subject in its setting and describing it in that place is a fuller way to present your topic.

Listen to some of how writer Brenda Z. Guiberson describes her subject, a sea turtle, as it reaches the ocean just after hatching on land.

> A gentle wave splashes across her back and carries her into the sea . . . the turtle knows how to paddle with her flippers and dive beneath the surface. She is still swimming hard when the sun moves into the sky. Every few minutes she comes up for a breath of air. Her eyesight is much better in the water. She sees a jellyfish, a starfish, and a barracuda with a big mouth. None of them see the turtle. Her white underside blends in with the shimmering white surface of the ocean.

Guiberson writes about the movement, the sights, and the sounds of the ocean. We can see the turtle in its setting. This helps us know the turtle better.

Where is your subject's place in the world. Can you help us see the subject in that special place by putting it there and describing it to the reader?

Using Strong Verbs

RESOURCE MATERIAL

❧ *Workshop* by Andrew Clements

DISCUSSION

It's easy for young students to fall into the trap of describing their subjects by relying on the passive verb *to be.* "A hammer is a very useful tool. It is used to pound nails." Whether students write about inanimate objects such as tools (as in the book used in this lesson) or live organisms, their writing becomes more vivid and lively when they use strong verbs to describe their subject in action.

HOW TO TEACH IT

The verb is the engine of a sentence. Today we are going to look at the difference strong verbs can make in writing. It might seem that the easiest way to describe something is simply to come out and say what it is. If you were writing a book about tools for younger readers, you might write, "A wrench is used to turn a nut. A drill is for making holes in wood. Pliers are a way to hold things together or to twist wire."

In his book *Workshop,* Andrew Clements uses action verbs instead of the passive verbs *is* or *are* to describe how the tools work, and this makes the writing more interesting. Let's compare his descriptions with mine.

A wrench <u>is used</u> to turn a nut.	Wrench <u>turns</u> the nut. Wrench <u>turns</u> the pipe. Wrench <u>loosens</u>, wrench <u>tightens</u>. Wrench <u>wrestles</u> metal.

Let's look at the verb I used and the verbs he used.
(Together, underline the verbs in each sentence.)

Clements uses four verbs to show the wrench at work: it turns, loosens, tightens, and wrestles. By the time we finish reading about the wrench, we get the idea of what it does. Can't you picture someone working hard to wrestle a nut loose from its hold on metal?

All of you have subjects you are describing. There are probably places where you are using the passive verbs—*is* or *are*—when you could use a stronger verb instead. You can liven up your writing by finding those sentences and rewriting them using stronger, action-oriented words. If you find a place where you want to try that but aren't sure how, let me know and we can look at it together.

Including Detailed Drawings

RESOURCE MATERIAL

❧ *A Medieval Feast* by Aliki

❧ *The Great Kapok Tree* by Lynne Cherry

DISCUSSION

Some students are comfortable pulling out facts from texts they read. But many students have a more visual orientation. When you see them poring over information books, it's clear that the lavish illustrations, not the texts, hold their attention. Later, when it's time for them to present their information, they are inclined to use visuals such as drawings, diagrams, charts, and photographs. We should show them how to do so.

True, some students may rely too much on visuals as a way to avoid writing. But we don't believe teachers should discourage students from using them. Rather, we need to guide them as they enrich their information writing with drawings or sketches to convey facts and details they have learned.

HOW TO TEACH IT

I want you to think about how your book or report will look to your readers. Page upon page of text can make for pretty dry reading. It's important to make your report or book as visually interesting as possible.

Drawings help a lot. Often it's easier and more effective to get across information in a drawing or illustration than by using words.

Let's take a close look at *A Medieval Feast*, an information book by Aliki. As I read it I want you to pay particular attention to the drawings.

(Read *A Medieval Feast* out loud. You could also use a visually rich book such as *The Great Kapok Tree* by Lynne Cherry.)

What struck you about these illustrations? Notice that the reader learns certain things in the drawings that don't get talked about in the text, and vice versa.

As you're working, start thinking about how you'll teach your reader what you've learned. Where would illustrations be most helpful? What medium might you use? Watercolor? Oil? Collage? How could you use drawings or other visual information to extend and explain what you have in your text?

Writing a Book Blurb

RESOURCE MATERIAL

ꙮ *Fig Pudding* by Ralph Fletcher

ꙮ *Mr. Putter and Tabby Pour the Tea* by Cynthia Rylant

ꙮ *Day of the Dragon King* by Mary Pope Osborne

DISCUSSION

When children write about books, they are engaging in informational writing. Here Lisa Siemens gives a new twist on the book report by having her students write a "book blurb" similar to the ones found on a book jacket. Lisa's class writes a blurb together before they each write one on their own.

HOW TO TEACH IT

Lisa says: "Last year, when my children published their first books, they decided to write 'book blurbs' for the back of each other's books. We began by examining a number of book jackets, reading the blurbs, noticing leads, similarities, and differences. I made overheads of the blurbs on the back of *Fig Pudding, Mr. Putter and Tabby Pour the Tea,* and *Day of the Dragon King.* Then we wrote one together for one of my student's books:

The Little Alligator by Thomas Miles
Can Chomper find a friend? Mile after mile, day after day, Chomper looked . . . but no luck. This is a story about loneliness and friendship. Even when Chomper finally finds a friend, there are still problems. This is a book for anyone who has ever searched for friendship.

"Because my students range in age from five to eight years old, the types of books they create can be anything from very simple repetitious texts to complicated fiction. Last year Geoffrey (6) was thoroughly excited by his newfound ability to write his own stories. In September he wrote a story about the seasons:

This is summer. A sun. A rainbow. Grass. And me. This is winter. A Snowman. A snowball. And me.

It was a very simple but elegant pattern, completely invented by Geoffrey. Sarah was in grade 3 and volunteered to write the blurb:

Seasons by Geoffrey Anderson
In this book, Geoffrey talks about the seasons. How will Geoffrey fit all the seasons in one book? Will he put two on one page? Will he put three on one page? Will he make up his own seasons? The only way to find out is to read *Seasons* by Geoffrey Anderson.

"I love the respect Sarah shows for Geoffrey in this review. She was just as inventive in her description as Geoffrey was in his creation."

Writing a Caption for a Photograph or Drawing

RESOURCE MATERIAL

❧ *The Great Fire* by Jim Murphy

DISCUSSION

It may seem odd to talk about photos and drawing in a book about nonfiction writing. But students increasingly live in a visual world. They investigate and learn from a number of nonprint sources. It's common for a student to visit an Internet site, download a photograph, print it, and incorporate it into the final report. Students need guidance so they can smoothly integrate these visuals into their nonfiction writing. Caption writing is another important kind of writing for this genre.

HOW TO TEACH IT

Let's take a look at *The Great Fire,* a book by Jim Murphy about the fire that destroyed much of Chicago in 1871. You'll notice that this book contains many drawings and a few photographs. Under each of these illustrations there is a short description that helps the reader understand what the photograph is about. That bit of writing is called a *caption.* These captions help readers understand the meaning of the illustrations.

Take a look at this drawing on page 32. It shows a fireman, and it looks like he's blowing some sort of horn. The drawing is confusing until you read the caption, which says,

> Even a small fire was a noisy experience, so fire marshals and steam engine foremen carried brass speaking trumpets to make their voices carry over the roar of the flames.

Many of you are working on a finished version of your information report. And many of you are planning to use photographs or drawings. These illustrations give you an important way to teach readers about your subject, but you can't expect the illustrations to stand on their own. You'll need to take time to write captions so the reader will understand the meaning of the drawings or photographs. A good caption is short—only one to three sentences. In that short space you need to

- Explain what the illustration shows. (Be specific!)
- Name the people.
- Tell why this is important to your topic.

Creating a Glossary

RESOURCE MATERIAL

🐾 *Geography from A to Z: A Picture Glossary* by Jack Knowlton

🐾 *Predator!* by Bruce Brooks

DISCUSSION

As students delve into a topic, they typically encounter a host of strange new words particular to their subject. A glossary helps readers understand these words. Students will encounter this feature in the books they read, and they can include a glossary in their finished writing. We believe this craft lesson would work equally well for middle school students.

HOW TO TEACH IT

During your research, you have probably come across new words you've never seen before. Let's say you're learning more about whales. You might read words like *baleen* and *ambergris.* Sometimes you come across a word you've heard before, but the author is using it in a new way. For example, *footprint* is a word you know, but the "footprint" of a whale is the particular way the water looks on the surface just above where a whale is swimming.

Many nonfiction authors understand that readers need help understanding these new words. They include a glossary that has these words with a brief definition of each one. *Predator!* by Bruce Brooks has a four-page glossary at the end.

Let's look at *Geography from A to Z* by Jack Knowlton, which is one long glossary on the subject of geography.

(Read *Geography from A to Z.* If kids already know it, reread a few pages.)

What did you notice about this glossary? I was struck by the fact that the writing that explains words such as *highland, isthmus,* or *volcano* is pretty short, usually two or three sentences, often shorter.

As you're researching, make a list of the specialized vocabulary you'll want your readers to know. Though you probably don't want to turn your entire report into a glossary, consider including a glossary at the end.

Teaching Information Through a Poem

RESOURCE MATERIAL

❧ "H20" by Ralph Fletcher (Appendix J)

DISCUSSION

One reason students' information writing is so sleep-inducing may be that they feel locked into only one way of writing—encyclopedia-speak—which happens to be the dullest. We need to teach students the conventions of content-area writing, but at the same time we need to show them cutting-edge techniques for making it come alive. In this craft lesson, we show students how to use a poem format to get across their information. One thing we like about poetry is that it requires students to teach information using few words.

HOW TO TEACH IT

Ralph Fletcher tells the story of the time he walked into a first-grade class and asked the students if they knew the chemical symbol for water.

"No," one boy replied. "We don't learn any chemistry until third or fourth grade."

Ralph thought that was funny. Everybody should know the chemical makeup of water! This incident inspired him to write this poem. (See "H2O" in Appendix J.)

Ralph Fletcher's poem has rhyme, and it has a finger-snapping beat, but it also teaches important information about water. As you work on your teaching books and reports, I want you to consider using some kind of poem to get across information to your readers. It's up to you whether or not your poem should rhyme. You might

- Put together a collection of teaching poems about your topic.

- Incorporate a poem into the body of your report.

- Use the poem as an introduction.

- Print the poem on the back cover or the jacket of your teaching book.

*T*he title for Anne Lamott's wonderful book on writing, *Bird by Bird,* came from a story about the author's brother. In school he was assigned to do a report about birds, and he avoided it. For weeks he kept procrastinating, putting it off. Finally his father sat him down and said, "Bird by bird, buddy. Just take it bird by bird."

That story reminds us of middle school students who are challenged to write nonfiction. Let's face it: school becomes difficult by fifth grade. The curricular demands are more intense. The demands in writing increase, too. Writing is seen less as an entity unto itself, and more as a vehicle for learning and demonstrating what has been learned. Teachers who want to devote class time to reading/writing workshop find themselves pressured to cover wide areas of the curriculum.

In grade 5–8 classrooms we see less expressive writing (fiction, narrative, poetry) and more content-related writing. This includes, but is not limited to, reports, term papers, persuasive essays, newspaper articles, business letters, and expository essays. We often find ourselves asking students to write about subjects (the Egyptians, ancient Greece, and so on) about which they have no firsthand knowledge.

Fortunately, middle-grade students have developed new strengths. They have become better critical readers, which can translate into making them better at rereading their own writing. Their vocabulary has strengthened, and they understand the range of purposes writing can serve. While younger students may focus on reporting the facts, middle-grade students are more able to report *and* react. They are equipped to identify a position, form an argument, or examine multiple angles. They will need all these skills and more to keep growing into strong writers.

Students at this age show a growing awareness of the world outside the self. They begin to develop strong opinions about controversial issues, such as testing on animals, for example. For years our son Robert was oblivious to the newspaper. Now, in fifth grade, he reads it hungrily while devouring his cereal. He reads about football, mostly, but it's a great start. He is drawn to statistics of the sports world.

But as students enter the middle school years they encounter the "great divide" in nonfiction writing. On one hand, they read numerous fascinating information texts, many of them written with zest, voice, and substance. They are pulled to emulate those texts, but we feel pressured to pull them toward more academic and, if we're honest about it, less interesting prose.

This great divide puts teachers in a quandary. Do we help our students write passionate informational writing even if it might hurt them on proficiency tests? Do we try to teach them the musty old five-paragraph essay—a form of writing that exists only in school? What is a teacher to do?

We believe that teachers should address this issue on two fronts. One of the main purposes of nonfiction writing at this age is to introduce students to academic writing. This is a real-world genre, with its own history, conventions, and the power to transform lives (or at least get a kid into college). It's no accident that students with strong academic writing skills usually do well in high school and college. Teachers need to help students become more skillful writers in this area.

But isn't something wrong when we find ourselves guiding students to write the kind of dry, voiceless prose we have no interest in reading? In fact, the whole genre of nonfiction has undergone dramatic changes in recent years. Tom Romano has opened a new frontier with his work on multigenre research. Students around the country are writing scripts for videos, creating hyper-portfolios, putting together PowerPoint presentations, starting on-line magazines, and so forth. In our districts, we can be advocates for this kind of writing. We can help revise writing curriculum so that it recognizes this shift.

The craft lessons in this chapter are geared toward a variety of subgenres, including persuasive, informational, biography, and expository writing. Some of them may seem to support more traditional academic forms of nonfiction, whereas others address more zestful and playful approaches. We don't attempt to address all the needs of middle school writers in these areas. Instead we've selected what we believe are the most useful strategies. We believe that these craft lessons will increase students' repertoire of strategies, giving them the freedom to apply them in their own work as they express themselves in various ways in the years ahead.

Exploratory: Activating Prior Knowledge

RESOURCE MATERIAL

❧ 20-page "blue book," one per student

DISCUSSION

You can see it in their slack body language: students passively receiving knowledge we want them to learn. It's important to remember that when students are beginning to research, they are not empty vessels. In fact, the students in our classroom already know a great deal about what they are learning. Unfortunately, curriculum isn't always designed to build on what they already know. This craft lesson suggests one way students can use a "learning log" to take an active stance as they investigate their subject matter. The craft lesson is adapted from a workshop activity run by Mary K. Healy.

HOW TO TEACH IT

Whenever you explore something, it's important to get in touch with what you already know about that topic. Today we're going to have some fun with this idea. I'm going to give you a quick assignment. Today imagine you are writing a report about astronomy. Open to the first page in your learning log. I'm going to give you exactly three minutes, and I want you to write down everything you know about astronomy. I'd suggest you use phrases, or fragments, instead of complete sentences.

(You may prefer to have students write on a different topic, or a subject students have been studying.)

Stop. Now get into groups of three. Take turns reading your list out loud. If someone in your group says something that you know is true, add it to your list. For example, let's say I'm in this group, and Maurice reads from his list that Galileo invented the telescope. Well, I knew that, but forgot to write it down, so now I can add it to my list. Make sure each person in your group gets a chance to read their list.

What did you notice? (Discuss.) Did you notice that some people in your group approached this subject in a different way than you did?

Remember: as you start researching your topic, it's probably not new to you. You probably know more about it than you think you do. It's well worth it to take a few minutes and jot down what you already know, so you can build on that as you keep learning.

Exploratory: Coming Up with Good Questions

RESOURCE
MATERIAL

&. None

DISCUSSION

Students expect teachers to provide questions that they in turn must answer. But nonfiction turns the tables: students must take a more active role and generate their own questions that will drive their research. This may feel like unfamiliar territory for some students, but we should do whatever we can to make them more active participants in this kind of writing.

HOW TO TEACH IT

You are just beginning your research. If you're learning about a topic that's new to you, it's important to *value your ignorance*. That sounds funny to say, but it's true. Pay close attention to the questions you have now, because chances are good that they are the same questions any other reader would have on this subject.

Let's imagine you're going to write a nonfiction piece about tattooing. What questions do you have? Get in pairs and talk about it for a minute.

(Brainstorm and discuss as a class.)

These are questions most readers would have:

Is it safe to get a tattoo?
Does it hurt?
Can you get it removed if you don't want it later?

These questions are good as starters. But you probably will want to revise your questions as you continue your research. After you have investigated tattooing, and answered those original questions, you might come up with new ones: What are the styles used by tattoo artists? What is the history of tattooing? You'll want to find the answers to those, too.

Start with what you don't know. As you begin your research, take a minute to generate the questions *you* have on your subject.

Exploratory: Making It Lively

RESOURCE MATERIAL

⁂ Excerpt from *Predator!* by Bruce Brooks (Appendix K)

DISCUSSION

When it comes to juicing up lethargic prose, skilled nonfiction writers have lots of tricks up their sleeves. As students try to create their own information texts, they need to spend time apprenticing themselves to the finest nonfiction writers around. This means giving both individual and class time for them to look thoughtfully at what these writers do to draw in the reader. Here we use an excerpt from a book by novelist-turned-nonfiction-writer Bruce Brooks. In this craft lesson we invite students to ponder an example of terrific nonfiction writing before they attempt to create their own.

HOW TO TEACH IT

With nonfiction writing, it's not enough just to teach the reader what you've learned. You've got to give your writing some oomph, some juice! Sometimes you find that the sentences you have written are sound asleep. Wake them up! If you don't, your reader will fall asleep, too.

I'd like you to take a close look at an excerpt from *Predator!,* a book by Bruce Brooks.

(Read aloud *Predator!* excerpt in Appendix K.)

Now, I'd like you to read it again. Read it silently to yourself.

(Students read.)

What did you notice? What made the writing interesting to read?

(Discuss with students. Make a list of what they notice about this excerpt. You may want to highlight the following: arresting choice of verbs, frame-by-frame slow motion, humorous asides, authentic details, and the author's voice.)

Look at this list. Remember: these are all things that you can do in your own writing to wake up your sentences, to make them come alive.

Exploratory: Writing a Flash Draft

RESOURCE MATERIAL

❧ Sample anecdote

❧ 4 × 6 index cards

DISCUSSION

An anecdote, small story, or brief scene can be used to convey a dynamic sense of a subject. We like to use the anecdote both as exploratory work and as a tool for crafting text. When used as part of the exploratory process, anecdotes help writers internalize new knowledge they are beginning to digest.

HOW TO TEACH IT

As you are researching your subjects, I can see that your notebooks are filling up with facts. It's important to be thinking about what those facts look like in the world of your subject. In other words, how can you bring these facts to life? For instance, let's say you are studying mushrooms and in your notes you have the following facts:

> mushrooms grow near pine trees
> mushrooms sprout in warm, moist weather
> mushrooms grow very fast

One way to practice thinking about what those facts mean is to embed an anecdote, a small story, or scene into your writing. Here's what it looks like:

> Deep in the forest animals scurry across the wet, spongy soil looking for insects and grubs that have surfaced with the newly fallen rain. The branches of the pine trees sweep the ground, making small dark caves around their trunks. It is warm and quiet, but still you cannot hear a mushroom as it quickly sprouts in the pine needle cave in the forest.

I call this a "flash draft," and it is used to help you imagine your subject in its natural surroundings. The flash draft you write may never end up in your final draft, but it can help you get to know your subject in a new way. Since anecdotes are meant to be short, I've put a stack of index cards in the writing area. Today, I'd like to ask each of you to take one and sometime during your research time, write a flash draft about your topic. Try it and see what you come up with.

Putting Tension in Your Title

RESOURCE MATERIAL

🔖 *The Perfect Storm: A True Story of Men Against the Sea* by Sebastian Junger

🔖 *The Bone Detectives* by Donna M. Jackson

DISCUSSION

The title is a highly condensed form of the subject itself. In the original *Craft Lessons,* we talked about how many students write titles that are no more than labels. These work fine as doors for the writer, but later they'll want to construct a title that works as a door for the reader. Titles are particularly important in nonfiction writing.

HOW TO TEACH IT

You've worked hard on your information report, but it's important to think about your title, too. Many writers use a "working title" as they write, and later revise the title to make it sharper and more interesting. The working title is often no more than a general label—"Hurricanes," "The Cheetah," or "Uranium." A working title like that can work fine as you explore your topic. But later, you may need to revise the title so that it will intrigue your reader.

You can do that in many ways. One way is to use a title that pulls the reader in two different directions. When Sebastian Junger wrote about the terrible storm that sank the *Andrea Gail* in the Atlantic Ocean, he decided to call his book *The Perfect Storm.* We think of "perfect" as a good thing and "storm" as dangerous, so at first those words don't seem to fit together. It makes us think. You want to open the book to find out what he means.

The same thing is true with a book such as *The Bone Detectives* by Donna M. Jackson. Everybody knows what a detective is, but the idea of a *bone* detective is somehow chilling. It makes you pause and wonder.

You can do this, too. Think about how you could put tension in the title of your nonfiction piece. For example, if you're writing about killer whales, you might use *Killer Whales* as a working title. Later you might decide that a title such as *Intelligent Assassin: The Killer Whale* would make your readers more interested.

Using Subheadings to Organize Information

RESOURCE MATERIAL

☙ Large easel with a blank chart

DISCUSSION

Many teachers would finger *organization* as the Achilles heel of their writers. Students do the hard work of researching, but it all falls apart when they try to organize their information into a coherent whole. A subheading is a simple tool when it comes to keeping each bit of information in its rightful place.

HOW TO TEACH IT

Does anyone here have boxes that hold various collections, such as cards, golf tees, bottle caps, or Beanie Babies? If you have lots of boxes, but forget to label them, it can be awfully hard to find a particular thing you're looking for.

The same thing is true with information writing. Readers appreciate it if the writer uses some kind of tag or label to tell them what's in a particular section of the text. That's where *subheadings* come in. Subheadings can help you organize your writing. They help the reader know at a glance what each part of your report will be about. And subheadings are a great tool for organizing the material as you gather it.

Let's imagine that you're writing a report about the tsunami or tidal wave. You're going to dig up lots of information, and you need to figure out a logical way to get it across to the reader. What would be the important parts?

(Brainstorm with students and write each item on a chart. Students may come up with categories similar to these:)

Where do tsunamis strike?	What can you do ahead of time?
How can you save yourself?	What causes a tsunami?
When do tsunamis tend to occur?	What is a tsunami, anyway?

As you write your report, each one of these could be a subheading followed by a paragraph, or several paragraphs, to explain the idea to your reader. Of course, these subheadings are probably out of order. What might be a better way to organize them? What should go first?

If you want to use subheadings, you'll want to:

1. Figure out your categories.
2. Figure out what information belongs in each one.
3. See where you need to add a new subheading to fill in a missing gap.
4. Decide what order they belong in.

Sharpening Your Lead

RESOURCE MATERIAL

❦ "Forms of Effective Leads" from *Writing to Deadline* by Donald Murray (Appendix L)

❦ Picture books showing various leads as models

DISCUSSION

Recently I asked Donald Murray about the difference between a lead and an introduction.

"Haven't you heard?" he asked with a chuckle. "We don't write introductions anymore; we write leads. Back in the old days we would tell readers what we were going to tell them, then we'd tell them, then we'd tell them what we just told them. That put readers to sleep. Now we realize that you've got to engage the reader by getting into the material right away. You can't wait."

Murray's wise words are worth keeping in mind (and sharing with students) as we explore ways to sharpen the lead.

HOW TO TEACH IT

Today I want you to think about your lead. This is the first tempting bite your reader gets of your writing. But if it's dull and tasteless, your reader will go off and read something else.

Here's a list of different kinds of leads. This was put together by writer Donald Murray.

(Read aloud "Forms of Effective Leads" from Appendix L. Make copies, if possible.)

Get into pairs, and talk about which one of these kinds of leads might work for your writing.

(Discuss with the class.)

I want to challenge you to come up with a strong lead for the piece you are working on. Here's one way you can strengthen the lead you have already written. Think of your writing as a river that goes over a big waterfall. Often when we write we start the piece too far "upstream" of the important information. You can sharpen your lead by starting it closer to the "waterfall"—closer to the most important information.

Writing a Narrative Lead

RESOURCE MATERIAL

✿ *She's Wearing a Dead Bird on Her Head!* by Kathryn Lasky

DISCUSSION

Human beings have been described as the "story species." And many students have a good sense of story. But when they move from narrative writing to information writing, it seems that they leave behind everything they once knew about story. That's too bad because skilled information writers draw on a wealth of fictional writing strategies (a sense of character, detail, suspense, and so on) to make their writing come alive. The following craft lesson draws on a strategy that many journalists have used to great effect—the narrative lead.

HOW TO TEACH IT

I know that many of you have been working hard to find a good lead for the nonfiction piece you are working on. Today, I'd like to explore something called the "narrative lead." We're going to take a close look at the first page of a book we all read earlier this year—*She's Wearing a Dead Bird on Her Head!* by Kathryn Lasky. This is a book about how the Audubon Society got started. Let's look at the first page:

> Harriet Hemenway was a very proper Boston lady—she never talked with her mouth full. But one day she almost did. Standing by the bay window in her parlor, she had just bitten into a jam cookie when her eyes sprang open in dismay. She gasped, leaned forward, swallowed, then turned to her parlor maid.
>
> "She's wearing a dead bird on her head!"
>
> Feathers on ladies' hats were becoming more and more popular. At first, hats had been decorated with just feathers, and then designers began to add pairs of wings. But this woman had an entire bird perched atop her hat! Harriet squinted her eyes as the lady of fashion walked proudly by.
>
> "Arctic tern, I believe," Harriet whispered.
>
> "Looks ready to fly away," said the parlor maid.
>
> "She won't," Harriet replied sadly.

A story or anecdote like this is a great way to start your writing. It lets us hear the characters speaking. It makes us feel like we're right there. If you're interested in writing a narrative lead, look through your notes and see whether there's a brief story that might work to kick off your piece. The story should be brief, no more than a paragraph or two.

Describing Your Subject

RESOURCE MATERIAL

≈ *Everglades* by Jean Craighead George (Appendix M)

DISCUSSION

The structure of school, where too many subjects are viewed as isolated curriculum, is probably what caused many of our students to become "compartmentalized thinkers." They think of using a metaphor while writing a poem, but it may not occur to them to use one while writing a story. In the same way they may use their powers of description while writing a narrative, but may not be aware of the value of this skill in nonfiction writing. It's important to do whatever we can to break down these arbitrary ways of thinking. Here we invite students to bring what they know about description to content-area writing.

HOW TO TEACH IT

When you teach what you know about a topic, you want your readers to be able to picture what you're talking about. If that's going to happen, you'll need to use all your powers as a descriptive writer.

Let's take a close look at *Everglades* by Jean Craighead George. This book is very informative, but at the same time, it is full of descriptive writing that makes us feel as though we're right there at the Everglades. Listen to this passage about how the Everglades were formed.

(Read passage. See Appendix M.)

What are some of the things that Jean Craighead George does well in this passage?

(Discuss.)

She uses the five senses. The river is warm. It gleams like quicksilver. It isn't noisy like other rivers. And you can almost feel the sharp points of the saw grass.

Also, she uses amazing verbs all through this book. On the next page she writes that the spoonbills "vacuumed the ponds and shallows with their sievelike bills."

Today I want you to think about your descriptive writing. Go back and reread your draft. Have you used your five senses? Have you used strong, interesting verbs? You might mark in the margin one place where you want to more fully describe what you're writing about.

Using Specifics with How–to Writing

RESOURCE MATERIAL

⁂ "Guide for a Clean Outhouse" by Marnie Wells (Appendix E)

DISCUSSION

How-to writing is perhaps the simplest, most common kind of expository writing. There will always be a need for clear writing that explains our increasingly complex world.

The example we refer to was written by an eighth grader. Marnie and her family had a camp with an outhouse on a small island. As with many fine pieces of writing, this one can be used to show students many things—writing with voice, using an introduction, including humor, and so on. It's probably important that this writing did not result from a classroom assignment. It had a true real-world purpose.

HOW TO TEACH IT

You've probably tried your hand at how-to writing before. Maybe you remember writing "How to Make a Peanut Butter and Jelly Sandwich," and the hilarious scenes that followed when somebody actually tried following your directions!

It's important to use specific details in *all* your writing. But using specifics in how-to writing isn't just a good idea, it's the law! Today we're going to talk about that.

Let's take a look at "Guide for a Clean Outhouse," written by Marnie Wells when she was in eighth grade.

(Read "Guide for a Clean Outhouse" in Appendix E.)

What did you think? What did you notice about her writing? (Discuss.)

You noticed that the author gives the reader specific instructions. She tells the reader exactly what kind of bugs to look for, and exactly how to get rid of them. She gives lots of examples.

Maybe you're working on a piece of how-to writing. Or maybe you're going to include some how-to information in your writing. Either way, don't take it for granted that the reader knows what you're talking about. Be as specific as possible, and make sure you don't leave out anything important.

Including Quotations

RESOURCE MATERIAL

&. None

DISCUSSION

Students need our help in bringing the human element into their information writing, especially when they are writing about subjects far beyond their own experience. Using selected quotations is a great way to do that. You may want to follow up this craft lesson with instruction about the proper use of quotation marks and related punctuation.

HOW TO TEACH IT

On August 12, 2000, the Russian submarine *Kursk* sank in the Barents Sea. You could write about that tragic event by using a number of facts and statistics. The *Kursk* was a nuclear submarine. It was 505 feet long, 60 feet high, and 30 feet wide. An explosion caused the sub to sink in 354 feet of water with 118 crewmen on board. All the crew members died. Those facts are important, but they don't really get down to the heart of what happened.

Later, divers entered the *Kursk*. They found a letter written by Dmitry Kolesnikov, one of the officers on board. Here's what he wrote:

> All the crew from the sixth, seventh, and eighth compartments went over to the ninth. There are 23 people here. We made this decision as a result of the accident. None of us can get to the surface . . . I am writing blind.

What did you find most compelling, the lists of facts or the letter? (Discuss.)

The truth is that it's not one or the other. When you write nonfiction you need *both* the facts and some memorable quotes like that.

Nothing is as powerful as the human voice. You can have a pile of wonderful statistics, but the spoken words of a flesh-and-blood person will bring alive your subject like nothing else.

Think of how a quotation might strengthen your writing. If you're researching, be on the lookout for a strong quotation you could use. You could use a quote from a person who was an eyewitness to what you're writing about. You could quote an expert or a person who could offer a fresh perspective. If you are writing a biographical sketch, consider quoting the person's own words.

Quotations can bring alive dry material. And a strong quote gives you a great way to begin—or end—your writing.

Revealing a Subject Through the Narrator's Eye

RESOURCE MATERIAL

🍂 *Pond Year* by Kathryn Lasky

DISCUSSION

Nonfiction writers sometimes choose to use narrative techniques as a way to teach about their subjects. One way to do this is to create a character and then, through first-person narrative, let the character bring his or her perspective to the topic.

HOW TO TEACH IT

You're all working hard to become experts in your subjects. When you are ready to write, you'll have choices to make about how to teach others what you have learned. Nonfiction writers sometimes choose to write in a straightforward report style. Other times they weave information into a story and use the story to entertain readers while teaching them some facts.

Today we're going to look at how a story can shape the way your reader learns about your topic. Let's consider what Kathryn Lasky does in her book *Pond Year*. She chooses to teach about life in a small pond by showing us how two young girls like to play and explore that pond over the course of a year. She chose to have the story narrated by one of the girls. Because a young child is telling the story we see the pond from a very particular point of view. Listen to this description of exploring the pond in June as the water starts to get warm:

> . . . we might sneak a wade. We don't call it wading, though. We call it dipping. We dip in our feet, and the water—all silty with swirled-up mud—leaves tan socks on them. . . . When we get tired of putting on our mud silk, we just stand still, letting the oozy bottom goosh between our toes, and we look for our tadpoles. We spot one. Through its transparent skin you see its front frog legs all folded up, almost ready to spring out.

The young narrator allows readers to explore the pond through the perspective of a child. Think of your topic. What perspective would you like your reader to have? Could you do that by creating a character who can teach us about it?

Making Transitions Between Paragraphs

RESOURCE MATERIAL

🎕 "A Monster Hurricane" from *Time for Kids* (Appendix N)

DISCUSSION

Organization is a *huge* issue for young writers. Students make a quantum leap when they figure out how to use particular paragraphs to develop particular ideas. But the resulting nonfiction writing is often a collection of choppy paragraphs, with large informational gaps between them. The next step involves showing these writers how to move smoothly between paragraphs. To be able to execute this sophisticated use of language, students need to see examples of how expert writers do it. The following craft lesson was written by Aimee Buckner. Aimee teaches fourth grade, but we believe this higher-level subskill is probably most applicable for middle and secondary school students.

HOW TO TEACH IT

"Sometimes, after my students have nailed the skill of writing grabber leads, I reread their writing and find the lead to be the only interesting sentence in their writing piece. Transitioning from paragraph to paragraph (or subject to subject) within a nonfiction piece is difficult for most of my students. Using subtitles helps, but I also like to focus on transition sentences—which will help them in all genres.

"That's when I pull out this article, 'A Monster Hurricane,' from *Time for Kids*. I have laminated a class set of this article to do the following work. My students read through this article about Hurricane Floyd. As they read, I ask them to highlight the sentences that really grab their attention. We then go back as a class and look at the article on a transparency, and we highlight the sentences the students found. Many of the sentences they choose do two things: one, they present a fact in an interesting way, and two, they are often a transition sentence. I point out and introduce the term *transition sentence*."

At this point, Aimee asks her students to look at their own pieces of writing. She challenges them to craft a transition sentence to help them bridge one paragraph to the next.

Using a Chart to Summarize Information

RESOURCE MATERIAL

❧ *1000 Facts About the Earth* by Moira Butterfield

❧ "Moons of the Planets" (Appendix O)

DISCUSSION

Students who delve into nonfiction writing typically suffer from information overload. So much to learn! So many sources! While juggling so many new facts, students may tend to revert to "list writing." Here we show them a tried and true way to get across important information in a concise format.

HOW TO TEACH IT

As you learn about your topic, think about how you're going to present it to your readers. Sometimes when you're writing factual information it can come across as a list: The Nile is the world's longest river. It is 4,145 miles long. The Amazon is the second-longest river in the world. It is 4,007 miles long. The Yangtze is the third-longest river in the world . . .

Sounds boring, huh? But you don't have to write it that way. A chart is a great way to present important facts like that. Take a look at this book *1000 Facts About the Earth* by Moira Butterfield. On page 43 you can see several charts about the earth, including one about the world's rivers. In one easy-to-read chart, she tells us all we need to know.

You can do the same thing. Let's suppose you're writing about the moons of the planets in our solar system. You could go through a laundry list with each planet and its moons. But a better way to handle it might be through a chart. Take a look at this.

(Show students "Moons of the Planets" in Appendix O.)

I want you to consider using a chart in your writing. Today when I confer with you, maybe you can tell me what information, if any, would lend itself to this kind of chart.

Varying Placement of Topic Sentences

RESOURCE MATERIAL

❧ "Placing a Topic Sentence" (Appendix P)

DISCUSSION

A disclaimer: we do *not* encourage you to overemphasize topic sentences in students' writing. Teaching students that every paragraph must have a topic sentence, and insisting that it must be the first sentence in a paragraph, will lead students to produce stilted, formulaic writing. Students' focus should be on their subject matter—not topic sentences—when they write. Many nonfiction writers don't consciously think about topic sentences when they write them.

But you probably can't ignore this idea, either. It may be more accurate to say that most paragraphs have one sentence that organizes or summarizes its contents. This is something we should make students aware of. In this craft lesson, we introduce students to the idea of a topic sentence, and we show how a topic sentence can be placed in different positions within a paragraph.

HOW TO TEACH IT

You may have learned about the topic sentence in a piece of writing. This sentence has more weight than the other ones. It is there to organize, or sum up, what the paragraph is about. Most paragraphs have one. Readers like to know what a paragraph is about. If you don't give them a sentence that summarizes the ideas, the reader may read your information and wonder, But what is this really about?

Today we're going to look at three paragraphs.

(Let students follow along as you read aloud "Placing a Topic Sentence" in Appendix P.)

Did you find any topic sentences in these paragraphs? Let's take these paragraphs one by one.

(Discuss.)

It's interesting that each of these paragraphs has a topic sentence, but that they are each in a different part of the paragraph.

Reread your writing. Can you find any paragraphs that don't have a topic sentence and need one? You may need to write one for that paragraph.

Defining New Vocabulary in Context

RESOURCE MATERIAL

❧ *Brain Surgery for Beginners and Other Major Operations for Minors* by Steve Parker

DISCUSSION

When students research a particular topic they often encounter new and specialized vocabulary. These words can be intimidating. You'll want them to feel comfortable using these new words in their writing. It may help to talk about ways other authors go about introducing special words to their readers.

HOW TO TEACH IT

As each of you were researching you began keeping lists of the new and specialized vocabulary you were learning. As you are writing, you'll find yourself wanting to use those new words to help your reader learn about your topic. These words may be new for your readers, too. They'll depend on you to use them in a way that they can understand. Let's look at one way a writer can do that. Here's a sentence from the book *Brain Surgery for Beginners* by Steve Parker:

> The lungs' main air pipes, the bronchi, branch many times until they form hair-thin tubes, terminal bronchioles. Those end in grape-like bunches of air bubbles, called alveoli.

Notice how the writer, Steve Parker, first introduces each part of the lungs by describing them in ways the reader will understand. Then he provides the technical terms. It's a lot easier for a reader to picture main air pipes that branch into hair-thin tubes than if the writer had gone directly to stating that bronchi branch into terminal bronchioles.

Since your job is to teach a reader, you have to be aware of how you are introducing new vocabulary. When you do, consider describing the concept in familiar terms first. Then give the technical term by setting it off in commas as this writer did.

Introducing and Using New Vocabulary

RESOURCE MATERIAL

❧ *The Honey Makers* by Gail Gibbons

DISCUSSION

Nonfiction writers trust that they can teach others their subjects. As students each develop a new area of expertise and set out to write about it, they learn to trust themselves as teachers. Here's another look at how students can first introduce new words, then proceed to use them with confidence.

HOW TO TEACH IT

Recently we talked about the technique of introducing new vocabulary by describing it first in common terms and then providing the technical term. Today I want to show you another way to introduce new vocabulary. In *The Honey Makers,* Gail Gibbons provides a straightforward definition of *metamorphosis.* Once she's done that, she trusts that readers have learned it. From then on she uses the word as she continues her discussion of how bee larvae change from pupae to full adult honeybees. Let's take a look:

> Little by little, the pupa changes. It begins to look more like an adult insect. This process is called metamorphosis. Queens develop in about 16 days from the time the eggs are laid. The metamorphosis of drones and workers takes about 21 to 24 days.

Once you've introduced a new word and explained it clearly, you can continue to use it as you continue writing about the subject. Take a look at your work, and consider whether you've clearly defined your terms, and whether you are using them to help educate your reader.

Using Anecdotes to Teach

RESOURCE MATERIAL

≈ *Deadly Animals*
by Martha
Holmes

DISCUSSION

Student nonfiction writing is notoriously flat. Students need strategies to help them take factual information and get it to stand up and come alive. Here we look at how writers embed anecdotes into finished nonfiction texts.

HOW TO TEACH IT

You've all written flash drafts as you learn about your topics. Today I want to talk with you about how writers often use an anecdote, small story, or brief scene in their final products.

Listen to this passage about the red piranha from *Deadly Animals* by Martha Holmes:

> Toward the end of the dry season, when the rivers are low, they are found together in great numbers. A boy driving his herd of cattle across the river doesn't realize the danger. The hungry fish smell the blood seeping from a recent wound on the cow's legs and dart toward her. She stumbles as they bite her legs, then more and more fish attack. Their feeding frenzy lasts only a few minutes. The cow has been completely eaten.

Martha Holmes could have chosen to state specific facts about the red piranha, but instead she decided to tell us a small story so we could see them in action. This anecdote about a boy and his cattle teaches us what piranha eat (cattle), what attracts them (blood), and how they feed (in frenzied groups and with speed).

The anecdote is a lively way to convey information. Sometimes you will find it best to state information straight out. Other times you may find that creating an anecdote is the best way to teach. To write your anecdote you will need a character, a setting, and some kind of action. Read over what you've written so far. Is there any place you could use an anecdote to liven up your writing?

Nonfiction Craft Lessons: Teaching Information Writing K–8

Integrating Personal Experience into an Expository Text

DISCUSSION

RESOURCE MATERIAL

❧ Excerpts from
Yukon River by
Peter Lourie
(Appendix Q)

Good nonfiction writing often reveals the relationship a writer has with his or her subject. Often it's not the subject that catches the reader's attention, but the writer's own interest in the subject. We once read an article on the history of Xerox machines by nonfiction writer David Owen. His passionate curiosity was so strong that we couldn't help but catch his enthusiasm for a subject that might have otherwise seemed boring. One way writers convey their connection to the subject is by integrating their personal experience into the expository text.

HOW TO TEACH IT

Many of you have personal experience with the topics you are studying. In fact, this experience may be the reason you have chosen to study a particular topic. One decision you make as a writer is whether or not to share your personal experience directly with a reader. In Peter Lourie's book *Yukon River,* he describes his journey down the Yukon as a way to teach us about this mighty river.

I want you to look at two passages from this book. In one instance, "A Fishing Camp," Lourie uses his personal experience to describe a salmon fishing camp. By contrast, the next passage provides a more detached explanation of the spawning practices of salmon. Each gets the job done, and they fit side by side in the reporting. Let's talk for a minute about the different effect each has.

(See Appendix Q for passages, or select passages from another text that students know well. Give students time to read and discuss the various effects of each.)

In the passage "A Fishing Camp," Lourie invites the reader to enter the camp with him. We feel like we are there, and in looking around we come to learn what it was like to live and work here. As you work on your writing, think of how you might include your personal experience as a way to teach the reader. Is there a place where your personal experience could enhance the writing?

Using Time as an Organizer

RESOURCE MATERIAL

❧ *Pond Year* by Kathryn Lasky

DISCUSSION

Learning how to wrangle a pile of information into a coherent whole can be a challenge even for experienced writers. Knowing how to find order is one of the skills of the nonfiction writer. There is no single best way to organize a set of facts; topics tend to lend themselves to particular approaches. One such approach is to use time as an organizer. If students are writing about topics that change or evolve over time, they may choose this approach as a way to highlight the life cycle of their subject.

HOW TO TEACH IT

If you are writing about something that grows and changes over time, you might want to consider using time as the main organizer for your subject. Just as stories have time lines where one event leads to another, nonfiction topics can be revealed by telling the story of how something changes or grows over time.

Kathryn Lasky is one nonfiction writer who has used this technique. She researched and wrote about life in a pond. The title of her book *Pond Year* gives a clue about how she chose to organize her information. In this book she gives her readers a view of the pond in each month of the year.

Once she knew she was going to organize her information by using a sort of time line, she still had to decide where to begin and where to end. Where might you begin if you were writing about this topic?

(Engage in a brief discussion and help students consider how different choices would lead to slightly different focuses.)

Lasky chooses to begin in April just as the pond is waking up from winter, and she ends in March with the promise of another spring. By beginning and ending there, I think she helps the reader focus on the way things spring to life in a pond.

Does your topic lend itself to a time focus? If you are getting ready to consider how to organize your research, ask yourself whether a time line approach would work best.

Establishing the Significance of a Fact

RESOURCE MATERIAL

⚓ None

DISCUSSION

"Establishing significance" probably sounds like a pretty highfalutin' goal for middle school kids. ("I'm just trying to establish a little discipline!" one teacher confided.) This subskill is challenging, but it's important that kids learn how to emphasize certain facts in their content-area writing. This craft lesson aims to at least get them thinking about including not just the "what" of a fact but also why that fact is important.

HOW TO TEACH IT

Your readers don't necessarily know which of your facts are there as background information, which ones are sort of important, and which ones are really important. You may need to explain so the reader understands which facts you want to emphasize, and why a particular fact is significant.

For example, let's say you're writing about Germany after World War II. You write,

> In December of 1990, Helmut Kohl won a decisive victory and became chancellor of Germany.

So what? True, this was more than just one more election, but don't assume that the readers know that. It's important to follow this sentence with another one:

> This was the first time all Germans had voted together for a leader since the country was divided in 1949.

That second sentence shows us the importance of this election by putting it in the context of German history.

Or let's say you're writing about the Battle of the Bulge, which was the last big German counteroffensive in World War II. You write

> The Germans suffered 220,000 casualties.

This sounds like terrible carnage, but readers are so used to reading huge numbers of dead during war they may get numb and just read on. You may want to make them ponder this number by adding,

> In this one battle the Germans suffered more casualties than all the United States casualties during the entire Vietnam War.

Go back and reread your writing. Do you have any important facts that are buried and not fully explained? Is there any place where the reader might not understand the importance of what you have written? You may want to add a sentence to explain why this is important.

Copyright © 2001
JoAnn Portalupi and
Ralph Fletcher.
Stenhouse Publishers

Listing Pros and Cons of an Argument

RESOURCE
MATERIAL

❧ "Arguments for
and Against
Capital
Punishment"
(Appendix R)

DISCUSSION

These next two craft lessons deal with persuasive writing. This is a new form of informational writing for middle schoolers, and they struggle with it. Here's a simple way they can use writing to brainstorm both sides of an argument before they start to write.

HOW TO TEACH IT

You are going to write a persuasive essay. That means you are going to argue for a certain point of view. How do you get started?

You might begin by taking a piece of paper and drawing a line down the middle. On one side of the paper write the word *pro*. On the other side write the word *con*. (You could also use *for* and *against*.) I suggest you use this paper to brainstorm arguments. Important: don't just write down the arguments that *you* believe. Put down all the arguments—even the ones you think are dumb.

For example, let's say you're going to write a persuasive essay about the death penalty. As you know, some states have a law that says a person who commits murder can receive the death penalty and be executed by the state. This is called *capital punishment*. Other states do not allow capital punishment. Here are some arguments on both sides of this issue:

(Show "Arguments for and Against Capital Punishment" in Appendix R. Take a few minutes to read and discuss.)

This is a very emotional and very complicated issue. I'd rather not spend class time talking about capital punishment right now. Instead, I want you to think about using this idea—a sheet listing pros and cons of an argument—for your persuasive essay. Take some time to list arguments. You absolutely do not have to use complete sentences.

After you finish, reread both lists. Which side has the longest list of good arguments? That may help you decide which side you want to take.

Airing the Opposing Point of View

RESOURCE MATERIAL

✍ "Preserving the Alaska National Wildlife Preserve" (Appendix S)

DISCUSSION

Let's face it: persuasive writing is a tough sell to kids of this age. It requires various skills that few young writers possess. Nevertheless, persuasive writing is a reality. It is one of the prompts on many state writing assessment tests. More important, it is a genre of nonfiction writing that remains important in the real world. Here we show students how to disarm the reader by airing the opposing side of an argument.

HOW TO TEACH IT

Today we're going to talk about persuasive writing. I want to start by having you think about how you persuade your parents when you want something from them. You know your parents are going to have some objections, so it's usually smart to mention them before your parents do.

Let's say you want to have a friend do a sleepover on a Monday night. You might say, "I know it's a school night, but we're going to be working on our science project together." You still might not get your parents to agree, but you've got a better chance now that you sound evenhanded.

This is also a smart strategy to use in persuasive writing. Let's take a look at this short essay. Take a moment and read this to yourself.

(Pass out copies of "Preserving the Alaska National Wildlife Preserve" in Appendix S.)

What did you notice? This person wants to keep the big oil companies out of the Alaska National Wildlife Preserve. But in the second paragraph he admits to the problem of oil shortages in America. In the long run, this strengthens his argument.

Think about this in your persuasive essay. Yes, you'll need to gather arguments that support your point of view, but it's also smart to give at least a little airtime to arguments on the other side. This will make you sound knowledgeable and fair.

Using Humor

RESOURCE MATERIAL

❦ *The Math Curse* by Jon Scieszka

❦ "Letters Between Lightning and Wind" by Ralph Fletcher (Appendix T)

DISCUSSION

It's tempting to dismiss humor in writing as silly and irrelevant. But we believe it is a mistake to do so. Recently Tom Newkirk has argued that parody is the central genre in the writing of boys. That is why books such as *Captain Underpants* by Dav Pilkey and the Jon Scieszka books have been so popular.

Humor is more than fluff. When students use humor in their writing, it's a sign that they feel comfortable with their material. This leads to lively writing with real voice. The challenge is to get students to avoid silliness and use humor in a way that strengthens the writing.

HOW TO TEACH IT

Nonfiction writing doesn't have to be dead serious. Today let's think about how you might use humor to make your writing more interesting. It's true that certain topics (war, endangered animals, and so forth) may not lend themselves to humor. But with many subjects humor can be a great way to get your reader to relax, have fun, and learn at the same time! The challenge is how to do it without getting silly.

The Math Curse by Jon Scieszka uses lots of humor. Let's revisit this book and see how he does it.

(Discuss.)

You'll notice that Scieszka uses math formulas and equations in lots of clever ways to give us a chuckle.

Now let's read "Letters Between Lightning and Wind" by Ralph Fletcher.

(Read to students. Make copies, if possible. Discuss.)

There's humor in these letters, but there's a lot of factual information, too.

Think about humor in your writing. Would it work? Use your imagination. The whole piece doesn't have to be funny, but you may find that using a bit of humor—a joke, a pun, or a funny drawing—brings it alive. Remember: even when you're using humor the factual information you teach has to be accurate.

Taking Poetic License

RESOURCE MATERIAL

✒ "The Salt Marsh" by Colin Drowica (Appendix U)

DISCUSSION

Poetic license—borrowing strategies from poetry—provides yet another way to energize tired informational writing. In this lesson we show how you might invite students to use sentence fragments to bring the reader deeper into their information.

Don't be surprised if some students resist this idea. In school we find a funny paradox about conventions of language. Teachers often lament that students are unable or unwilling to write a sentence correctly. Yet when we invite them to break the rules, they have trouble doing it!

HOW TO TEACH IT

While you've been in school you have learned the rules of how to write a word, a sentence, a paragraph, and so forth. Those rules are important because they allow your reader to enter into the piece you are writing. But sometimes a writer will deliberately break one of those rules. I'd like you to read a bit of information writing that was produced by a fifth grader named Colin. Colin does something very interesting in his writing.

(Make enough copies of "The Salt Marsh" by Colin Drowica in Appendix U and pass them around so every student has one. Read the piece out loud.)

Okay, now I'd like you to get into pairs and quietly read it again. What do you notice about the writing? Where does it surprise you? Read it and quietly discuss this with your partner.

(Students read and discuss.)

Let's talk about this piece. How about the first paragraph, the introduction? These first three sentences work fine enough. But what about the second paragraph? What did you think of that? Why do you think Colin wrote it this way? What effect did it have on you when you read it?

(Discuss.)

Colin used *sentence fragments*. This is a technique you sometimes find in poetry. For me, these fragments felt different from the rest of his piece. It almost felt as if I were there in that marsh with him. As you write, ask yourself whether you want to use fragments the way Colin did. You don't want to overuse this technique. A few sentence fragments in the right place will go a long way.

End with a Bang!

RESOURCE MATERIAL

🦋 "The Attack on Pearl Harbor" (Appendix V)

DISCUSSION

Endings are tough for students. This partly stems from the fact that they "frontload" so much information that by the end of the piece, they have run out of things to say. As a result, their pieces often end weakly. Here's one way to help them spruce up their endings.

HOW TO TEACH IT

You have been working on crafting strong leads for your nonfiction pieces. But actually the ending is as important as the beginning. The ending is the part that will echo in the ear of the reader when he or she is finished. As I read some of your pieces it feels like you have run out of gas by the very end. Let's see if we can work on the ending.

As you learn about your topic, and think about how to present it to readers, you'll have lots of information you want to communicate. But you don't have to share it all at the beginning. If you have a great quote, an amazing fact, or a powerful story, you may want to hold it back so you can use it for your ending.

Let's imagine you are doing a historical piece about the attack on Pearl Harbor that took place in 1941. Here are some facts you might have dug up. Take a moment and read this.

(Read out loud "The Attack on Pearl Harbor" in Appendix V.)

Many of you have already learned about this attack. But as you read this page, which facts struck you? Get with a partner and discuss that.

(Discuss in small groups.)

Which parts did you identify? The part that struck me the most was when Emperor Hirohito of Japan said,

> "I fear that all we have succeeded in doing is to awaken a sleeping giant." He was referring to the United States, and he was right. This attack brought the United States into the war. And the U.S. navy hunted down and destroyed thirty-two of the thirty-three Japanese ships that launched the surprise attack.

If you were writing this, you might do well to end with a powerful detail like this.

Today, as you write, think about your ending. You may want to consider saving some fact, quote, story, or image so you can use it to fashion a strong ending.

Questions and Answers

*T*he first three questions are excerpted from our first book, *Craft Lessons: Teaching Writing K–8*. We think they are just as applicable to this book.

Where do these craft lessons fit into my language arts program?

These craft lessons are designed to fit into the mini-lesson component of the writing workshop. But don't limit your thinking to this one time of the day. You'll find that they can also be helpful during a one-to-one writing conference. These lessons will help you think about individual students' writing in fresh ways. If the moment is right, seize the opportunity to introduce a craft lesson right then and there.

The lessons can also enrich the book discussions you have with students. In fact, much of what students learn about the craft of writing takes place *outside* the writing workshop at other times of the day: during literature circles, large-group book discussions, or one-on-one reading conferences. Writing workshop becomes the time for students to act on the information they are learning about craft by trying it out in their own writing.

Is it best to assign these craft lessons or leave them optional?

The point can be argued both ways.

Assign them: yes! These strategies are too important to be left up to the students' whim. If we make them optional, students won't take them seriously, and some students will never try them out. Certain kids will simply never see the power of using a narrative lead, for instance, unless we ask them to try it at least once.

Assign them: no! If we do that, it becomes *our* workshop instead of theirs. A student will no longer sit down and consider, What am I working on now? Instead he'll look up and think, What does she want us to do today?

This is a judgment call only you can make. We know excellent teachers who would line up on both sides of the question. We believe that a strong classroom environment incorporates a great deal of student choice. This includes the decision about what writing strategy to use, and when to use it.

There may be occasions when you want all students to try out a particular strategy. But in general, these craft lessons should be presented as options for students to use if and when they see fit. Ideally, your classroom has the kind of environment where you put forth lots of rich writing ideas and your students are willing to try them out.

What about students who don't take up the invitation?

Not all young writers will be ready to try each new element of craft the day you present it. But there are ways to keep the idea alive so that when they *are* ready, they'll be reminded to give it a try.

One way is to create a place in the classroom that reminds students to explore the elements of craft. For example, you might design a bulletin board that lists the various kinds of endings, and ask students to add models of each as they find them in the books they are reading, or as they experiment in their own writing. This sets up an "after-image" of your lesson, and will help extend its usefulness to more students in the workshop.

There are other ways to encourage more students to attempt the lesson you are teaching. Let's face it: teaching a mini-lesson can be like lighting a match—it burns brightly for a little while but quickly burns out. The danger in mini-lessons is mentioning instead of teaching.

You can reinforce a mini-lesson by returning to the element of craft at the end of the writing time. Designate a corner of the blackboard where the craft element gets highlighted, and have students sign their names after they try it in their writing. At the end of the writing time, remind students what you discussed with them during the mini-lesson. Find out which students tried out the craft element in their own writing, and start your share session by asking a few of those students to read their writing aloud.

You might also use a large easel pad to record discussions and demonstrations. This allows you and your students to refer to earlier lessons about craft and apply them at a later time. It also provides a personalized record of the craft lessons you have taught over the course of the year. Next year's class will be unique and will influence what you teach about craft and the way you teach it. Still, it will be useful to have an archive of your own lessons to draw from.

I have trouble finding some of the titles you use in the craft lessons. What do you suggest?

Don't despair if you can't find a particular book. Many teachers have their own favorite books. As you read through the individual craft lessons you may find that another, similar book comes to mind. Don't hesitate to replace the one we selected with one of your own choice. The best book to use in a craft lesson is the one you and students already know and love.

You may still want to use the book we suggest in the craft lesson but find that it is out of print. We have tried to refer to books that are in print, but unfortunately, that's no guarantee that each one will still be in print a year or two from the date this book is published. You may be able to find the book in your own library, during a library sale, or at a used bookstore. Check the following web sites to help you find out-of-print books:

- Amazon.com
- www.powells.com
- www.bibliofind.com

Couldn't students work on their nonfiction writing at home?

When we went to school, we did almost all our "report writing" at home, with volumes of the World Book Encyclopedia opened on the kitchen table. We believe that this kind of writing is too important to be relegated to homework. Parents can still have an important role in research and, later, in providing an audience for the finished product. But we encourage you to have students do the lion's share of their information writing in school where you can guide them as they explore this challenging genre.

Do you recommend that students work on information/nonfiction writing during writing workshop, or at a separate time?

If possible, we suggest you let students engage in this kind of writing during writing workshop. Writing workshop shouldn't be limited to narrative writing. We think it is robust enough to incorporate many different kinds of writing, including nonfiction.

What would it look like to have students working on information/nonfiction writing during writing workshop?

Well, for one thing, the teacher would bring in a ton of nonfiction texts to support and sustain this kind of writing. The workshop structure would reflect a nonfiction focus. Mini-lessons would focus on researching, using an index, focusing on a topic, interviewing, plus all the craft lessons set forth in this book. During writing time students would be engaged in researching, doing exploratory writing, and generating interview questions. In one-to-one conferences, the teacher would encourage students to teach what they are learning about their subjects. The teacher might help students with organizational issues, and would try to guard them against trying to write about huge, unmanageable topics. During share time, students could teach the class what they are learning, where they are running into snags, and so on.

It sounds like you recommend that students write nonfiction as part of a whole-class genre study. But couldn't they also explore it on an individual basis?

Certainly. It depends both on the teacher's preference and the age of the students. In a first-grade class, you might see all sorts of genre writing going on at one time. Mark is writing a true story about going to a football game. Amy is writing a fairy tale. Brenda is writing a teaching book about dolphins. That may be workable because at that level we hope to simply introduce these students to these various kinds of writing.

As students get older, each genre becomes more sophisticated and demanding. As teachers we expect more from their nonfiction writing. In some upper-grade workshops, students explore nonfiction writing on an individual basis. But some upper-grade teachers lead students in a whole-class genre study in nonfiction writing. (We also know many primary teachers who have had great results by moving students as a class from writing stories to "teaching books.")

But doesn't the idea of a whole-class genre study contradict the idea of choice in the writing workshop?

No. Student choice in writing is important, but it was never meant to be some kind of blank check for students to do whatever they want. Choice is, as Tom Newkirk has pointed out, negotiated between the teacher and student. You might well opt to have all students work on nonfiction writing at the same time. But if you do so, we suggest that you give students as much choice as possible. They're all writing nonfiction, but each student gets to choose his or her topic, to decide what angle they want to take, and so forth.

Time is in such scarce supply. I know student choice is important, but it's natural to use nonfiction to cover some of the many curriculum demands in science and social studies. Is it okay to assign topics in this case?

Lucy Calkins once remarked that when teachers ask students to write about a curriculum area, we are "trying to kill two birds with one stone. Unfortunately, we often end up killing both birds." In other words, what we end up with is neither real research nor real writing.

To answer this question: yes, many teachers will challenge students to work on nonfiction writing connected to the curriculum. But beware of going back to the time when teachers assigned every fourth-grade student to write a state report that had to include the capital, major cities, state flower, state bird, state motto. . . . Such assignments are usually a recipe for dead, voiceless writing. When we give students an umbrella topic on which to write, we should give them as much choice as possible within that common topic. That way each student can find her own angle, or rope off her own area of expertise that is distinct from the other students.

Some of these craft lessons deal with helping students organize their writing. What's wrong with giving kids an outline to help them stay organized?

It's tempting to give students a preset, detailed outline to help them organize their nonfiction writing. But there's a danger of making your students dependent on such forms. Whatever outlines or organizers we use, we should stand back and ask ourselves, Will they need the same detailed outline next time they write? Are we moving students toward becoming more independent writers who can devise their own schemes of organization? These two questions should guide us.

What about fictionalized nonfiction? Is it a good idea to encourage students to blend these two genres?

Yes and no. On the one hand, just try to separate these two genres when you're working with kindergarten and first graders! Young children love to start with some factual bit of knowledge and weave it among fascinating fictional details. This may be because of underdeveloped boundaries between reality and fantasy, or it may come from the models they have around them. (Consider how common it is for young children to read stories or watch movies in which animals talk!)

As students get older, their knowledge of distinct genres grows and they more consciously decide to write in one or the other. Now students are able to deliberately blur the boundaries and do it well. A student writes a poem that teaches about the electoral system. Another embeds her research on raising wolf pups into a fictional story set in the far North. There is nothing wrong with supporting or even encouraging students to write in this direction. If they want to do so, we should let them apprentice themselves to professional writers such as Jean Craighead George or Kathryn Lasky, who do this well.

Still, we advocate for some time in each school year when students set to the task of writing straight nonfiction. We believe it is a distinct skill to organize factual information and to write engagingly about it. Students will be called to write in this manner throughout their school careers and beyond. As teachers, it is our responsibility to help them learn to be comfortable and knowledgeable in the world of writing nonfiction.

How do you handle plagiarism—students copying whole passages of text from a book into their own writing?

Use a gentle touch. Research has shown that many kids don't fully understand plagiarism. Students often don't understand the difference between copying a passage and putting an idea into their own words. We have to teach them.

Plagiarism is often a symptom of a deeper problem—they aren't yet comfortable enough with their information to write clearly, and with voice. This may be an indication that they need to do more exploratory writing so they can make all these new facts and concepts part of who they are.

I like the idea of encouraging my students to use exploratory writing to think their way into their subject matter. But how do I assess that when it comes time to evaluate their nonfiction work?

Remember that exploratory writing represents a student's first-draft, fragile thinking on a subject. You might think of exploratory writing as a window into your students' thinking. Read it, enjoy it, respond to it. But don't correct or grade it. That's the surest way we know to shut down this kind of tentative writing.

Instead, exploratory writing becomes part of the overall assessment of the student's work. Let students know you expect them to use this kind of writing as a tool for learning. You may ask that they include it in a portfolio as evidence of their research process. This tentative write-to-learn kind of writing will show you the thought process that led to the final draft, and help you more thoroughly assess a student's final draft.

Our students need to be prepared for expository prompts on the statewide writing assessment. How will a nonfiction study prepare them for this?

When we work with students across a range of genres, we help them learn to identify how one kind of text differs from another. When it comes time to write to a prompt, students must recognize what the prompt is asking for. Is my task to write a story, a descriptive paragraph, a piece of exposition?

When confronted with an expository prompt, students face the challenge of generating ideas and then organizing them to convey a coherent point of view to the reader. Students who have been involved in nonfiction study have experience in sifting, sorting, and ordering information. They have handy tools at their fingertips: using exploratory writing, trying various forms of maps or outlines, generating questions a reader may have. They know that main ideas must be accompanied by supporting details and specific examples. All these skills will serve them well during crunch time.

As with any performance-based writing assessment, the best preparation is time spent writing coupled with time talking about what works for individual writers. If our classrooms are places where students write, reflect on their writing processes, and talk about what constitutes good writing, they have just about all they need to succeed in the testing situation. The final piece of support comes in sharing information about the testing situation itself. Savvy teachers spend time talking about specific prompts and give students time to rehearse under "test conditions." That way they can bring all they know about nonfiction writing to the testing situation.

But as teachers we must lift our sights beyond the pressures and particulars of the state assessment test. We live in an information world. This kind of writing will have far more significance to our students' lives than how well they perform on these tests. When we help students become more skilled at juggling information and writing about the real world, we are giving them tools that will serve them for the rest of their lives.

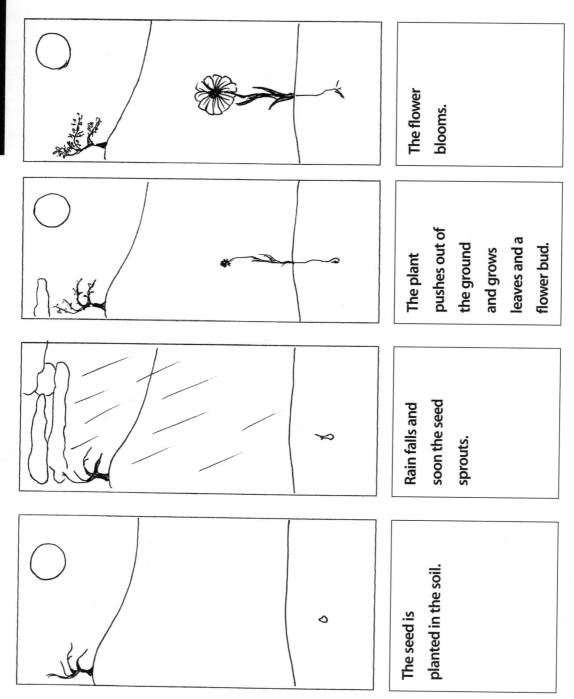

The flower blooms.

The plant pushes out of the ground and grows leaves and a flower bud.

Rain falls and soon the seed sprouts.

The seed is planted in the soil.

Nonfiction Craft Lessons: Teaching Information Writing K–8

All abawt thee oyl sPil

Some of thee anamolse did
from the oyl Spil.

thee Worter wosint Blue It
Wos Black

I Wish Exxon wod cleyn
up the werter.

I reyly fyl
Mad

and aingry

. . . ryly aingry!

All About the Oil Spill

Some of the animals died
from the oil spill.

The water wasn't blue it
was black.

I wish Exxon would clean
up the water.

I really feel
mad

and angry

. . . really angry!

Lauren Loewy (first grade)

Brainstorming

Beginning

Middle

End

Brainstorming	Beginning	Middle	End

Tsunamis are tidal waves caused by earthquakes deep in the ocean

How to prepare

Occur mostly in the Pacific

Cause great damage in low-lying areas

Scientists trying to develop better warning systems

Move very fast

Slow as they move toward shore

What to do—move to higher ground

Guide for a Clean Outhouse

"A clean outhouse is a happy outhouse."

Introduction

This pamphlet is your guide to quick and easy outhouse cleaning.

Your sparkling, fresh-smelling outhouse can be the envy of all your neighbors.

Guests will remark that your privy is the best that they have ever visited.

If you want to hear all sorts of wonderful things about your outhouse, read the

following pages carefully and enjoy with the author's compliments . . .

Section One: When Is My Outhouse Dirty?

Your outhouse is always dirty, however, the untrained privy-cleaner needs to

know what to look for. Listed below are some signs of a dirty outhouse.

On the ceilings:

(insects including) ants, spiders, daddy-long-legs, wasps, hornets, mosquitoes, ter-

mites, etc.

(signs of insects including)

cobwebs, eggs, nets, excrement, etc.

On the seat area:

empty beer/soda cans (you get the idea)

On the floor:

sticks, pine-needles, hemlock needles, leaves, mouse turds, dead animals, dirt, sand,

toe-jam and any of the things listed under "On the ceiling" or "On the seat area."

Now that you know the signs of a dirty outhouse, let us proceed to the second

section . . .

Section Two: The Daily Clean

A daily clean is essential for every outhouse that is used regularly. It takes no more than five easy steps and 4.25 minutes.

Materials: broom

1. Remove broom from behind cabinet.
2. Sweep all cobwebs and foul things from ceiling.
3. Sweep the floor, making sure to get everywhere.
4. Sweep everything out the door.
5. Replace broom behind cabinet.

Section Three: The Monthly Clean

The monthly clean is extremely important to the maintenance of your outhouse. It takes 30–45 minutes. Sometimes, professional privy-cleaners can be hired to do this kind of cleaning, but it is generally expensive.

Materials: scrub brush, bucket, disinfecting detergent, gas mask, rags, water

1. Remove everything from the outhouse including rugs, cots, oars, tents, axes, linoleum, extra toilet seats, etc.
2. Sweep all debris from ceiling and walls. A scrub brush and detergent may also be necessary.
3. Using scrub brush and detergent, clean the toilet seat and seat pedestal thoroughly. Rinse and dry.
4. Scrub cabinet. Rinse and dry.
5. Scrub floor. Rinse and dry.
6. Using broom and/or scrub brush, clean *all* floor coverings and dry with rags.
7. Wipe cobwebs, dirt, dust, lime, etc. from everything that was removed from the outhouse as a result of step 1.

8. The outhouse may need some time to dry and air out so go take a bath while you're waiting.

9. Replace everything in the outhouse.

10. Preach constipation.

Section Four: General Tips

- Don't be afraid to get down on your hands and knees on the floor with the scrub brush if necessary.
- Always leave the door open in nice weather to guarantee that your privy gets sufficient airing (especially if there were beans at the last meal).
- Clean often to avoid build-up of dirt, insects, odor, etc.
- Don't just chase insects away. Kill them.
- If you see scattered lime, brush it into the hole.

Now that your outhouse is the envy of all your neighbors, remember to keep it that way!

Marnie Wells

Chess is one of the oldest games around. People have played it for thousands of years. Today, people play it all over the world. Young children play it and grown-ups play it. Chess is a battle between two armies, black and white. Each player tries to capture the opponent's king while at the same time, protect his or her own. There are many pieces to help you. Each army has a queen, two rooks, two bishops, two knights, and eight pawns. Learning how to move these pieces can be challenging. Chess is a great game and is not difficult to learn. The first thing to know is how each player moves on the board and how they capture other players. You'll want to know a few other things like how to defend yourself from a checkmate and how to protect your king by castling. Once you start to play, you will never stop learning how to play it better. That's because there is always something to learn or invent about how the pieces work together. If you like playing with your friends you might want to try playing in a chess tournament. The USCF (United States Chess Federation) sponsors scholastic tournaments for school age children. At tournaments you get to play new players. Playing different players allows you to learn more strategies. If you play in a tournament you will earn a rating that tells you and other players how strong of a chess player you are.

Chess is one of the oldest games around. People have played it for thousands of years. Today, people play it all over the world. Young children play it and grown-ups play it.

Chess is a battle between two armies, black and white. Each player tries to capture the opponent's king while at the same time, protect his or her own. There are many pieces to help you. Each army has a queen, two rooks, two bishops, two knights, and eight pawns. Learning how to move these pieces can be challenging.

Chess is a great game and is not difficult to learn. The first thing to know is how each player moves on the board and how they capture other players. You'll want to know a few other things like how to defend yourself from a checkmate and how to protect your king by castling. Once you start to play, you will never stop learning how to play it better. That's because there is always something to learn or invent about how the pieces work together.

If you like playing with your friends you might want to try playing in a chess tournament. The USCF (United States Chess Federation) sponsors scholastic tournaments for school age children. At tournaments you get to play new players. Playing different players allows you to learn more strategies. If you play in a tournament you will earn a rating that tells you and other players how strong of a chess player you are.

Saltwater Taffy

Saltwater taffy has been around a long time. One legend teaches that it was named after a vendor on Atlantic City's Boardwalk who had his supply of taffy damaged by a storm tide in the summer of 1883. But even without the name—saltwater taffy—it was around long before that. Some say that taffy was invented from toffee recipes that colonists brought over from England. When making the toffee they found that when they pushed and pulled the sticky substance it began to change. Instead of toffee, they had taffy!

Rabbits

Rabbits are mammals. They have long floppy ears, and they have lots of soft fur. They are quiet. Lots of people think rabbits are furry and cute, but many farmers consider rabbits pests because they eat crops and cause a nuisance.

There are several different kinds of rabbits, including the jackrabbit, the cottontail, the snowshoe, and the common domesticated rabbit. Snowshoe rabbits eat mostly vegetables, but adult snowshoe rabbits sometimes eat mice. The cottontail rabbit will stay motionless to avoid being seen. This rabbit can swim well, and often gets away from enemies by plunging into a lake or stream. Jackrabbits are the fastest rabbits around. They can achieve a top speed of about 45 mph!

Lots of people have domestic rabbits for pets because they are sweet and nice. Domestic rabbits warn one another of danger by thumping on the ground with their hind feet. Rabbits like to hop around. People like to give each other bunnies on Easter. Some people carry a rabbit's foot, and think that it gives them good luck. Domestic rabbits have been used in many scientific experiments. Some domestic rabbits' furs have been sold under the trade names of arctic seal, clipped seal, and lapin.

Appendix 1

Commas in a List

Bats are gentle. Bats are intelligent. Bats are fascinating.

Bats are gentle, intelligent, and fascinating.

Bats can hibernate in caves. They can hibernate in mines, too. Sometimes they hibernate in other shelters.

Bats can hibernate in caves, mines, or other shelters.

Bats roost in caves. Sometimes they roost in mines, too. Buildings are a place they roost. Bats can roost in hollow trees.

Most bats roost in caves, mines, buildings, or hollow trees.

Italicized text from Bats! *by Laurence Pringle*

H20

The recipe

for water is

the same as

it's always been

two parts

hydrogen

one part

oxygen.

Two to one

that's the rule

to make a water

molecule.

Ralph Fletcher

Predator!

All right, you're a leopard and you've been very clever and you've cornered an eighty-pound baboon with three-inch fangs and frightened him into an adrenaline-stoked frenzy of hatred. Great! Now what, hotshot? Remember— you're supposed to be *happy* about this; you've worked hard to put yourself in this position.

What you do, if you are a leopard, is simple. You fake a step forward, inducing the baboon to make a do-or-die lunge at your eyes with those fangs. Then you pull back. The fangs click together a half-inch in front of your face, and before the stumbling primate can open his mouth again, you swing your right leg sharply from the shoulder and clout him on the side of the chest. He flies ten feet and lands in a tangle of broken ribs and crushed organs, and you heave a sigh: whew! Not that you ever doubted your superior strength, or your speed, or your craftiness. But all the same, those fangs, if they *did* get your eyes . . .

The sternest fact of a predator's life is this: if you are going to go around getting dangerous animals into a fight for their lives, you'd better have the stuff to put them on ice.

from Predator! *by Bruce Brooks*

Forms of Effective Leads

News. Tells the reader what the reader needs to know in the order the reader needs to know it: who, what, when, where, why.

Anecdote. A brief story that reveals the essence of your subject.

Quotation. A quote lead can give additional authority and a fresh voice to the story.

Descriptive. Sets the scene for the story.

Voice. Voice establishes the tone of the story.

Announcement. Tells the reader what you are going to say.

Tension. Reveals the forces in the story and sets them in motion.

Problem. Establishes the problem that will be solved in the article.

Background. Provides the background so the reader will understand the importance of the story.

Historical. Places the story in a historical context.

Narrative. Establishes the story as the form of the article.

Question. Involves the reader in the fundamental issue of the story.

Point of view. Establishes the position from which the reader will be shown the subject.

Reader identification. Shows readers how the story relates to them.

Face. Gives the reader a person with whom to identify during the reading of the story.

Scene. Sets up an action between participants in the story that reveals the central meaning of the article.

Dialogue. Allows the story's meaning to come from the interaction of principal people in the story.

adapted from Writing to Deadline *by Donald Murray*

Lake Okeechobee filled to its brim and spilled over. The spill became a river that seeped one hundred miles down the peninsula from Lake Okeechobee to the Florida Bay. It was fifty miles wide and only six inches deep in most places.

This river did not chortle and splash. It did not crash over falls and race. It was a slow river that gleamed like quicksilver. We know it today as the Everglades.

Into the shallow, warm river came tiny one-celled animals and plants. They lived and died and made gray-green soil on the bottom of the river. Saw grass took root in the soil.

The grass prospered. When the winds blew, the saw grass clattered like a trillion swords. Each sword was edged with cutting spines. Of the larger animals, only the leathery alligator could walk unharmed among the terrible spears of the saw grass.

from Everglades *by Jean Craighead George*.

A Monster Hurricane

In one city after another, the streets fell silent. Jacksonville, Florida. Charleston, South Carolina. Wilmington, North Carolina. These usually bustling seaside cities became ghost towns under gray skies. Empty homes with boarded-up windows lined silent, rain-drenched streets. Miles of cars snaked slowly away, looking for higher ground and shelter. Nearly 3 million people along the East Coast had been ordered to pack up and get out last week. It was the biggest evacuation in U.S. history.

What evil force could possibly drive so many people from their homes? Monster Hurricane Floyd, a 600-mile-wide superstorm. Fearsome Floyd first whipped the islands in the Caribbean Sea with 155-mile-per-hour winds. Then it hovered offshore near Florida, scaring coastal residents silly as it whirled its way up the nation's eastern shoreline.

Florida and Georgia were spared the worst of the storm, although Disney World was forced to close for the first time in history! The hurricane gave birth to at least six tornadoes that struck the Carolinas, along with up to 16 inches of rain. Floyd's eye, or center, finally hit land just before 3 A.M. on September 16, bringing 110-mile-an-hour winds to a North Carolina town with the perfect name for such a scary landing: Cape Fear.

"They talk like this one is going to be pretty mean," said Terry Hurley, as he hurried his family into a Wilmington emergency shelter. The Hurleys had waited out previous hurricanes at home, but they weren't taking any chances with Floyd. "It's got everybody shook up."

So How Bad Was It?

At least 17 deaths were blamed on Floyd. By the end of last week, officials were still figuring out how much property the storm had destroyed, and expecting even more flooding. All along the East Coast, school days and workdays were canceled or cut short. More than a million people were without power; tens of thousands slept in emergency shelters; and water sloshed everywhere. But the storm could have been much more deadly.

The last disastrous hurricane, Andrew, in 1992, killed 26 people and caused $25 billion in damage. Floyd did less harm, partly because everyone had plenty of warning. Floyd also kept to a mostly offshore path. But many meteorologists saw its incredible size and strength as proof that we are in an era of stronger and more frequent hurricanes.

Is the World Heating Up?

One vital ingredient of any hurricane is warm water to fuel its whipping winds. Since 1900, the average temperature of the Atlantic Ocean has risen about 2 degrees.

Some scientists blame this temperature boost on global warming. Their theory: carbon dioxide and other gases that pollute the atmosphere trap the sun's heat close to the earth's surface. Others say the current hurricane cycle is the result of climate patterns. Whatever the cause, most experts agree warmer oceans mean trouble. "If temperatures continue to increase," says Thomas Karl, director of the National Climate Data Center, "I'd bet that tropical storms and hurricanes are going to be stronger."

Living on the Edge

What makes this prediction even scarier is the fact that so many people live near the beach. Half the U.S. population lives within 47 miles of a coast. By 2010, 3 out of every 4 people are expected to live that close to the ocean.

When big storms hit, homes built on the shoreline may be smashed into matchsticks. The cost of insuring and rebuilding such homes is extremely high. Storm experts say it's not worth the cost, or danger, and building near the shore should be outlawed.

"It's now pretty clear that a hurricane will come every year," says Tim Eichenberg of the Center for Marine Conservation. "To continue to allow people to build right on beaches is just asking for trouble."

The trouble is not over. When Floyd faded, Gert—the next hurricane—was already hovering in the middle Atlantic. Weary, soaked East Coast residents wondered whether they would meet monster storms Harvey, Irene, Jose and Katrina. How many more before this year's hurricane season ends on November 30?

Time for Kids, Sept. 24, 1999

Moons of the Planets

Mercury	None
Venus	None
Earth	Moon
Mars	None
Jupiter	Europa
	Ganymede
	Callisto
	Io
	8 others
Saturn	Mimas
	Enceladus
	Tethys
	Diore
	Rhea
	Titan
	14 others
Uranus	Oberon
	Titania
	Umbriel
	Ariel
	Miranda
	10 others
Neptune	Triton
	7 others
Pluto	Charon

Placing a Topic Sentence

At the End of a Paragraph

Spiders construct ingenious webs that work as nets to capture prey. Some spiders build underground burrows with a trapdoor that allows them to snatch insects unlucky enough to wander past. Other spiders disguise themselves as ants in order to get close to their victims. Still others have learned how to capture fish in streams and ponds. No wonder that spiders have been called the greatest predators in the insect world.

In the Middle of a Paragraph

Politicians tend to oversimplify America's drug problem, and how to deal with it. Stopping drug use is a lot more complicated than putting "Just Say No" posters in high schools. However, nobody would deny that the use of illicit drugs continues to be a serious problem in America's high schools. Between 1992 and 1996 the use of marijuana among high school seniors increased from 32.6 percent to 44.9 percent. Among the graduating class of 1996 over 50 percent of the students had used an illicit drug, continuing an upward trend from 40.7 percent in 1992.

At the Beginning of a Paragraph

Ted Williams was the greatest hitter of all times. In 1941 he finished the season batting over .400, a feat that no other player has equaled ever since. Opposing managers so feared Williams that they devised the "Ted Williams Shift" in which all the infielders moved to the right side of the diamond to stop him from pulling the ball. Williams, or Teddy Ballgame as he was called, slugged 521 homeruns during his career for the Boston Red Sox. That's an impressive figure, but imagine what the total would have been if he had not lost four prime years of his career to military service.

A Fishing Camp

Ernie and I pulled over at a native fishing camp and found long poles that had been set up as fish racks for drying salmon fillets. The salmon run was over, and no one was around. The log cabins, their roofs packed with earth and moss, were old and sturdy. We went in one of the cabins, and I was struck by the idea that we could stay there all winter long if we wanted to. No one would bother us. I could almost smell salmon cooking on the old stove (p. 17).

Salmon Run

The king (chinook) salmon makes one of the longest spawning runs of any fish in the world. From the middle of July to the end of August, she leaves the Bering Sea and starts up the Yukon, to spawn thousands of miles upriver. She eats nothing on her way, yet she averages about fifty miles a day against the swift current, passing all kinds of dangers, such as nets, logjams, and bears. At last she arrives at the very stream in which she herself was born. How she finds her way back to this spot is one of the wonders of nature. Some say she recognizes her birthplace by smell. Perhaps it is a chemical recognition, a kind of memory. Nevertheless, if she survives the hazards in the river, she will always reach her birthplace to spawn (p. 18).

from Yukon River *by Peter Lourie*

Arguments for and Against Capital Punishment

Pro

Will deter criminals from
killing again.

Life imprisonment is very
expensive to the state.

Punishment (death) fits the
crime (killing).

Gives comfort to families of
the victims.

New DNA testing makes it less
likely that innocent people get
executed.

Con

Studies show that it does
not stop criminals from
committing murder.

Innocent people have been put to
death and it's too late to appeal.

An "eye for an eye" is barbaric—
the state becomes no better than
the murderer.

Some criminals serving a life
sentence for murder have found
ways to commit good deeds.

Executions such as by lethal injection
are "cruel and unusual punishment,"
which is not allowed under our
Constitution.

Preserving the Alaska National Wildlife Preserve

Recently we have heard politicians argue that it's time to allow oil companies to dig for oil in the Alaska National Wildlife Preserve. Some argue that the need for oil is more important than environmental concerns. Others believe that exploration in this place can take place without undue harm to nature. But opening up this pristine wilderness would be a gigantic error. And once the mistake has been made, it cannot be undone.

It's true that the United States has a growing need for oil. Our population has risen, and in the north, at least, each newly constructed home needs fuel for heating. We don't produce enough oil in America. In fact, during the past ten years our dependence on oil from the Middle East has increased. When trouble erupts in this unstable region of the world, and the oil supply is threatened, the price of oil spikes higher. Little wonder that some people believe this problem can be solved by tapping American oil reserves.

But digging in the Alaska National Wildlife Preserve would be a major mistake. This is the place where the caribou, and many other animals, mate. It is a crucial spawning area for whales and seals. Digging up this area would destroy the fragile ecology of many endangered species.

Digging for oil in this area would take five or six years before we would see any results. Even then the experts predict that this area would yield about a million gallons of oil per day. This may seem like a lot until you consider that the United States imports about ten million gallons of oil every day. The truth is that we could save at least a million daily gallons or more through conservation efforts. Politicians don't like to talk about conservation because it seems to go against the "American way of life." Carpooling, lower house temperatures, and higher gas prices may be annoying, but they are small prices to pay for leaving this pristine wilderness area intact.

Letters Between Lightning and Wind

My beloved Wind,

Why have you been ignoring me? You must admit that I have an electrifying personality! I even amaze myself sometimes! Today I sent out a huge lightning bolt with enough voltage to light up the city of Rochester, New York!

My battery never goes dead! Did you know that I send out 10,000 lightning bolts around the world on a single day!

Do you like bowling? I can curl up into a fiery sphere (it's called ball lightning) and roll right down Main Street! That really shakes up the neighborhood! Maybe we could go out on a date.

Last time we spoke you criticized me for starting fires and shocking people. I promise I'm going to be a lot better about the electrocutions. Like today on a soccer field these mothers were talking, right? I could have zapped them but instead I put a jolt into the ground beside them. You know what happened? The women's hair stood straight up! They got freaked out and ran to their cars, but nobody got hurt.

Wasn't that nice of me?

I apologize about starting the fires, but that's where I need you, sweetheart! See, I figure we could work together. You could swoop in and blow out lots of fires as soon as they start! By the way, I've changed my name. How do you like it?

Sincerely,

Zeus

Dear Zeus,

Stop bothering me. Stop sending me letters. I don't like you. I will never—EVER!—go on a date with you! Who do you think you are? I have seen the way you show off every time there's a T-storm, sending off those ridiculous tongues of electricity. Plus you electrocute people! You start fires! You set a horrible example for children! Go bother someone else!

Re-volted (get it?),

Wind

from "Weather Letters" by Ralph Fletcher

The Salt Marsh

My class and I went on a two day trip to Caumsett (New York). We did many different and fun activities there. The one activity I found the best was the salt marsh.

Step after step your feet sink more into the wet mud. Sweet salt on the skinny rods of grass. Blowing in the wind. Derooted plants. Ice cold water. Warm and smelly mud. Little crabs crawling out of their holes hunting for food. A raccoon scrambling through the grass. That is what it is like in a salt marsh.

While we were in the salt marsh our naturalist told us that marshes are endangered land. That also means that the animals' habitat is endangered since many animals live there. Two famous New York airports were built on marsh land. During this trip I learned that the salt marsh is a crucial ecosystem where the land meets the sea. I believe that we must do whatever we can to preserve the precious salt marshes.

Colin Drowica (grade 5)

The Attack on Pearl Harbor

Early in the morning of December 7, 1941, Japanese submarines and carrier-based planes attacked the U.S. Pacific fleet at Pearl Harbor. Nearby military airfields were also attacked by the Japanese planes. The damage was devastating: 8 American battleships and 10 other naval vessels sunk or badly damaged, almost 200 American aircraft destroyed, and 3,000 naval and military personnel killed or wounded. The attack marked the entrance of Japan into World War II on the side of Germany and Italy, and the entrance of the United States on the Allied side.

When asked if this attack was a success, Emperor Hirohito of Japan was quoted as saying: "I fear that all we have succeeded in doing is to awaken a sleeping giant." He was referring to the United States, and he was right. This attack brought the United States into the war. And the U.S. navy hunted down and destroyed thirty-two of the thirty-three Japanese ships that launched the surprise attack.

Soon after the attack, U.S. President Franklin D. Roosevelt appointed a commission of inquiry to investigate which U.S. military officers had been responsible for the Japanese raid on Pearl Harbor. The commission's report found the naval and army commanders of the Hawaiian area, Rear Admiral Husband E. Kimmel and Major General Walter C. Short, guilty of "derelictions of duty" and "errors of judgment." These officers were forced to retire. Other later inquiries, however, had different conclusions. The Congress of the United States, in an effort to dispose of the controversy, decided on a full, public investigation after the war.

Copyright © 2001 JoAnn Portalupi and Ralph Fletcher, Stenhouse Publishers

References

Adler, David A. 2000. *America's Champion Swimmer: Gertrude Ederle*. Illus. Terry Widener. San Diego: Harcourt Brace.

Aliki. 1983. *A Medieval Feast*. New York: Crowell.

Allen, Judy. 2000. *Are You a Snail?* Illus. Tudor Humphries. New York: Kingfisher.

Arnosky, Jim. 1997. *All About Rattlesnakes*. New York: Scholastic.

Asch, Frank. 2000. *The Sun Is My Favorite Star*. San Diego: Harcourt Brace.

Barton, Byron. 1988. *I Want to Be an Astronaut*. New York: Crowell.

Blumberg, Rhoda. 1993. *Bloomers*. Illus. Mary Morgan. New York: Bradbury.

Brooks, Bruce. 1991. *Predator!* New York: Farrar, Straus, Giroux.

Bunting, Eve. 1990. *The Wall*. Illus. Ronald Himler. New York: Clarion.

Butterfield, Moira. 1992. *1000 Facts About the Earth*. New York: Scholastic.

Calkins, Lucy, and Shelley Harwayne. 1987. The Writing Workshop: A World of Difference. (Videotape.) Portsmouth, NH: Heinemann.

Cherry, Lynne. 1990. *The Great Kapok Tree*. San Diego: Harcourt Brace.

———. 1994. *The Armadillo from Amarillo*. San Diego: Harcourt Brace.

Christian, Peggy. 2000. *If You Find a Rock*. San Diego: Harcourt Brace.

Clements, Andrew. 1999. *Workshop*. Illus. David Wisniewski. New York: Clarion.

Cole, Henry. 1995. *Jack's Garden*. New York: Greenwillow.

Collard, Sneed B. III. 1997. *Animal Dads*. Illus. Steve Jenkins. Boston: Houghton Mifflin.

Davis, Katie. 1998. *Who Hops?* San Diego: Harcourt Brace.

———. 2000. *Who Hoots?* San Diego: Harcourt Brace.

Dewey, Jennifer Owings. 1998. *Poison Dart Frogs*. Honesdale, PA: Boyds Mills Press.

Ehlert, Lois. 1990. *Feathers for Lunch*. San Diego: Harcourt Brace.

Eyewitness Junior series. New York: Knopf.

Fanelli, Sara. 1995. *My Map Book*. New York: HarperCollins.

Fleming, Denise. 1996. *Where Once There Was a Wood*. New York: Holt.

Fletcher, Ralph. 1995. *Fig Pudding*. New York: Clarion.

Freedman, Russell. 1987a. *Indian Chiefs*. New York: Scholastic.

———. 1987b. *Lincoln: A Photobiography*. New York: Clarion.

———. 1994. *Kids at Work: Lewis Hine and the Crusade Against Child Labor*. New York: Clarion.

George, Jean Craighead. 1995. *Everglades.* New York: HarperCollins.

George, William T. 1989. *Box Turtle at Long Pond.* New York: Greenwillow.

Gibbons, Gail. 1995a. *Knights in Shining Armor.* Boston: Little, Brown.

———. 1995b. *Sea Turtles.* New York: Holiday House.

———. 1997. *The Honey Makers.* New York: Morrow.

Gibson, Marie. 1998. *The Pet Tarantula.* Auckland, NZ: Shortland.

Golenbock, Peter. 1990. *Teammates.* Illus. Paul Bacon. San Diego: Harcourt Brace.

Guiberson, Brenda Z. 1996. *Into the Sea.* Illus. Alix Berenzy. New York: Holt.

Hiscock, Bruce. 1999. *The Big Tree.* Honesdale, PA: Boyds Mills Press.

Hodge, Deborah. 1997. *Whales.* New York: Scholastic.

Holmes, Martha. 1991. *Deadly Animals.* New York: Atheneum.

Jackson, Donna M. 1996. *The Bone Detectives.* Boston: Little, Brown.

Jenkins, Steve. 1999. *The Top of the World: Climbing Mt. Everest.* Boston: Houghton Mifflin.

Junger, Sebastian. 1997. *The Perfect Storm: A True Story of Men Against the Sea.* New York: Norton.

Knight, Margy Burns. 1996. *Talking Walls: The Story Continues.* Illus. Anne Sibley O'Brien. Gardiner, ME: Tilbury House.

Knowlton, Jack. 1988. *Geography from A to Z: A Picture Glossary.* New York: Crowell.

Krull, Kathleen. 1996. *Wilma Unlimited: How Wilma Rudolph Became the World's Fastest Woman.* Illus. David Diaz. San Diego: Harcourt Brace.

Krupp, E. C. 1993. *The Moon and You.* New York: Macmillan.

Kumin, Maxine. 1984 [1968]. *The Microscope.* Illus. Arnold Lobel. New York: Harper & Row.

Lamott, Anne. 1994. *Bird by Bird.* New York: Pantheon.

Lasky, Kathryn. 1995a. *Pond Year.* Illus. Mike Bostock. Cambridge, MA: Candlewick Press.

———. 1995b. *She's Wearing a Dead Bird on Her Head!* New York: Hyperion.

London, Jonathan. 1993. *Voices of the Wild.* New York: Crown. OP.

Lourie, Peter. 1992. *Yukon River.* Honesdale, PA: Boyds Mills Press.

Martin, Jacqueline Briggs. 1998. *Snowflake Bentley.* Illus. Mary Azarian. Boston: Houghton Mifflin.

Miller, Debbie S. 1994. *A Caribou Journey.* Boston: Little, Brown.

Meltzer, Milton. 1993. *Gold: The True Story of Why People Search for It, Mine It, Trade It, Steal It, Mint It, Hoard It, Shape It, Wear It, Fight and Kill for It.* New York: HarperCollins.

Murphy, Jim. 1995. *The Great Fire.* New York: Scholastic.

Murray, Donald. 1984. *Write to Learn.* New York: Holt, Rinehart. OP.

———. 2000. "Forms of Effective Leads." In *Writing to Deadline.* Portsmouth, NH: Heinemann.

Myers, Walter Dean. 1995. *One More River to Cross: An African American Photograph Album.* San Diego: Harcourt Brace.

Osborne, Mary Pope. 1999. *Day of the Dragon King*. Minneapolis: Sagebrush.

Pallotta, Jerry. 1996. *The Freshwater Alphabet Book*. Watertown, MA: Charlesbridge.

Parker, Nancy Winslow, and Joan Richards Wright. 1987. *Bugs*. New York: Greenwillow.

Parker, Steve. 1995. *Brain Surgery for Beginners and Other Major Operations for Minors*. Illus. David West. Brookfield, CT: Milbrook Press.

Parsons, Alexandra. 1990. *Amazing Snakes*. New York: Knopf.

Penner, Lucille Recht. 1991. *Eating the Plates: A Pilgrim Book of Food and Manners*. New York: Macmillan.

Peterson, Cris. 1999. *Century Farm: One Hundred Years on a Family Farm*. Honesdale, PA: Boyds Mills Press.

Pringle, Laurence. 2000. *Bats! Strange and Wonderful*. Honesdale, PA: Boyds Mills Press.

Raschka, Christopher. 1998. *Arlene Sardine*. New York: Orchard Books.

Rockwell, Anne. 1998. *Our Earth*. San Diego: Harcourt Brace.

Ryan, Pam Muñoz. 1997. *A Pinky Is a Baby Mouse, and Other Baby Animal Names*. New York: Hyperion.

Rylant, Cynthia. 1994. *Mr. Putter and Tabby Pour the Tea*. San Diego: Harcourt Brace.

Scieszka, Jon. 1995. *The Math Curse*. New York: Viking.

Settel, Joanne. 1999. *Exploding Ants: Amazing Facts About How Animals Adapt*. New York: Atheneum.

Siebert, Diane. 1991. *Sierra*. New York: HarperCollins.

Silver, Donald M. 1998. *One Small Square*. New York: McGraw-Hill.

Simon, Seymour. 1995. *Wolves*. New York: HarperTrophy.

Sis, Peter. 1996. *Starry Messenger: A Book Depicting the Life of a Famous Scientist, Mathematician, Astronomer, Philosopher, Physicist, Galileo Galilei*. New York: Farrar, Straus, Giroux.

Solheim, James. 1998. *It's Disgusting and We Ate It! True Food Facts from Around the World and Throughout History*. New York: Simon & Schuster.

Time for Kids. 1999. "A Monster Hurricane." Sept. 24, Vol. 5, No. 3.

Turner, Ann. 1985. *Dakota Dugout*. New York: Macmillan.

Weiss, Nicki. 1990. *An Egg Is an Egg*. New York: Putnam.

Wells, Robert E. 1993. *Is a Blue Whale the Biggest Thing There Is?* Morton Grove, IL: A. Whitman.

Wick, Walter. 1997. *A Drop of Water: A Book of Science and Wonder*. New York: Scholastic.

Wright-Frierson, Virginia. 1996. *A Desert Scrapbook: Dawn to Dusk in the Sonoran Desert*. New York: Simon & Schuster.

———. 1999. *The North American Rain Forest Scrapbook*. New York: Simon & Schuster.

Wu, Norbert. 1993. *Fish Faces*. New York: Holt.

Zinsser, William. 1988. *Writing to Learn*. New York: Harper & Row.

Topic Index